Ironman 70.3
Training for the Middle Distance

Ironman Edition

IRONMAN 70.3
TRAINING FOR
THE MIDDLE DISTANCE

Henry Ash / Marlies Penker

Meyer & Meyer Sport

IRONMAN., **70.3**™ and M-dot are registered trademarks of the
World Triathlon Corporation

Original title: Ironman 70.3 – Triathlontraining für die Mitteldistanz
© 2008 by Meyer & Meyer Verlag

Translated by Heather Ross

British Library Cataloguing in Publication Data
A catalogue record for this book is available from the British Library

Ironman 70.3 – Training for the Middle Distance
Maidenhead: Meyer & Meyer Sport (UK) Ltd., 2009
ISBN: 978-1-84126-342-7

© 2009 by Meyer & Meyer Sport (UK) Ltd.
2nd edition 2011
Auckland, Beirut, Budapest, Cairo, Cape Town, Dubai, Indianapolis,
Kindberg, Maidenhead, Sydney, Olten, Singapore, Tehran, Toronto
Member of the World
Sports Publishers' Association (WSPA)
www.w-s-p-a.org
Printed by: B.O.S.S Druck und Medien GmbH, Germany
ISBN: 978-1-84126-342-7
E-Mail: info@m-m-sports.com
www.m-m-sports.com

Contents

Foreword

Welcome. This book is a thorough guide to preparing for the most popular triathlon racing distance in the world. Spawned from the renowned Ironman Triathlon series, Ironman 70.3 is booming internationally because these triathlons, raced at half the Ironman distance over 70.3 miles, provide the challenge of long-distance triathlons but are not as intense a training venture as the full Ironman distance.

Having personally coached hundreds of athletes successfully at this distance, from beginner to world champion, I can tell you that Henry Ash and Marlies Penker do a fantastic job of skillfully directing you through the intricate steps of preparing for this endurance challenge. Starting your event well prepared physically and mentally will build your confidence and put you at ease, allowing you to enjoy a day that will forever be a memorable milestone in life. Ash and Penker present their information in an easy-to-read, systematic manner.

Whether you are just starting out their or looking to up your game, you will find this guide to be an essential resource in your training library. Get ready to get in the shape of your life!

Lance Watson
* Founder, LifeSport Coaching
* Triathlon Olympic Gold Medal Coach
* Ironman Champion Coach

1   Introduction

1.1   Ironman 70.3 – One step at a time

"The road to Ironman fame is 70.3 miles long"

This phrase sums up the special challenge of the Ironman 70.3. And it is just one more leap from the Ironman 70.3 to its big brother, the Ironman 140.6, which is the ultimate endurance-sporting accolade.

Ironman ist a high-quality, recognizable name for a challenging event that, each year, attracts more people who want to conquer it to become known as hardcore athletes.

Ironman 70.3 does not only mean mastering a long triathlon consisting of a 1.2 mile swim, a 56 mile bike-ride and a 13.1 mile run; Ironman embodies the "calculated adventure" par excellence, the struggle against water, wind, the course, and yourself. It means uncertainty as to how those 70.3 miles will affect our bodies, the countless highs and lows, the doubt and hope, the moments of strength and weakness that every athlete goes through on their way from start to finish.

Ironman also embodies motivation, willpower, perseverance, energy, strength, flexibility, the need to be active and the dream of finishing, all qualities that are required in everyday life. The opportunities for transferring these qualities to the Ironman are therefore unlimited.

So why race 70.3 miles all in one go?
Do you too dream of completing an Ironman 70.3 or another medium distance triathlon?

Then all you need is good health and passion...

...for the multi-faceted endurance sport, consisting of swimming, cycling and running.

www.chris-herzog.ch

In order to attain your Ironman goal, it is *not* essential to:

- Be young or unattached

- Train 20 hours or more per week

- Be a semi- or full-professional athlete

This is exemplified by the following people's success stories:

46-year-old Dan, who before turning 45 had never exercised regularly apart from a few bike rides.

Patricia, now 42, who took up triathlon because she wanted to get fit. She caught the Ironman bug four years ago.

36-year-old Doris was an enthusiastic spectator of the Ironman Austria who hung up her ice hockey skates in order to take up the triathlon.

40-year-old Oliver, whose principal motivations to train are the challenge, his enjoyment of sport and the testing of his performance limits, still manages to be competitive with an average of 8-9 training hours per week.

1.2 The keys to success

"It is better to start slowly than to drop out quickly!"

By using realistic training suggestions, specific examples and other tips, we intend to give you the keys to succeeding in the Ironman 70.3. The 70.3-mile course is purely theoretical. In competition, many factors can cause the 1.2-mile swim to become a few hundred yards longer, and almost nobody finds the ideal line during the 56-mile cycling component or the 13.1-mile running course.

Our daily swimming, cycling and running training should be equally flexible. Who knows that better than Henry after 25 years of triathlon training! This makes our Ironman 70.3 training a little more accessible.

M. Nüsken

With this book, "Ironman 70.3," we – Henry and Marlies – would like to lead you on your personal Ironman journey. The countless facts, tips, suggestions and hints are intended to ensure that you retain or enhance your enjoyment of endurance sports as well as master your journey to the Ironman 70.3 as safely as possible. Unfortunately, we cannot completely save you from slight detours.

We hope that you too will experience the deep satisfaction of completing an Ironman 70.3 successfully and in good health. We therefore wish you much fun and enjoyment, for we are absolutely certain that success is sure to follow.

www.cep-sports.com

2   The Appeal of the Ironman 70.3

The fascination of the Ironman 70.3 can be summed up in two sayings and with a few important facts:

If you want to do triathlon, then do the Olympic distance, but if you want to find a new life (and yourself), then do an Ironman.

> *You can buy a house, but not a home.*
> *You can buy a bed, but not sleep.*
> *You can buy a clock, but not time.*
> *You can buy a great bike, but not an IRONMAN!*

More facts that make the Ironman 70.3 appealing:

* The many hours of training
* Getting to know your own body
* Discovering and raising your performance limits
* Struggling against problems and obstacles during preparation
* The length of the course and the weather
* The uncertainty of the race's outcome
* The different nature of swimming, cycling and running
* Struggling to overcome challenges in the water, on the bike and on the running course

- The satisfaction of reaching the long-awaited and eagerly anticipated finish line
- Justified pride at having accomplished your goal
- The sublime feeling of having conquered the 70.3 mile course
- Increased self-confidence, physical well-being and physical capacity
- The certainty that one has done something out of the ordinary
- Mastering the challenge you have set for yourself
- The affirmation of your will power, endurance and perseverance

The fascination with the Ironman 70.3 is closely linked to swimming, cycling, as well as running the course length. The Olympic discipline, on the other hand, is considered to be a standard triathlon competition that can easily be mastered with the correct training. However, it is precisely those extra miles on the bike and on foot that make the difference and give the Ironman its mythical status. They account for the uncertainty and thrilling anticipation typically felt in endurance events (flow) as we head toward the finish. Can we can get our legs, mistreated during the cycling, to cover the 13.1 miles on foot? After the 60.3 miles, will our burning muscles be able to cover the remaining 10 miles? Will we avoid "hitting the wall" until after the finish, or it will be waiting for us at the next aid station? In an Ironman 70.3, we never know what will happen until we actually cross the finish line.

If you are already feeling bad after swimming, you have a problem.

It's normal to feel exhausted after the cycling.

But it's not normal if you don't feel dead after 70.3 miles!

Most Ironman 70.3 participants ask themselves just before or during the race, "Why am I doing this? Do I have to? Can't I live without the Ironman 70.3?" Many curse themselves, the race, and everything around them and vow never to put themselves through this torture again.

However, after a short recovery phase at the finish, nearly all paticipants become repentant liars, and in typical Ironman fashion, bask in the positive memories and start to plan their next Ironman 70.3, the little man's title of nobility.

Here the common saying, "the journey is the reward," applies. Positive memories of the training for swimming, cycling and running are awakened.

The goals that we were really seeking were overcoming obstacles; the countless hours in the sun, rain, wind and snow; the positive, sociable and exciting hours spent swimming, cycling and running; these are the things that make an Ironman out of a triathlete.

The rich experience of these hours of training give us the opportunity to let our minds wander, but also to socialize and enjoy the beauty and changing seasons of nature. All of this makes the Ironman an event that provides a quality of life that we are not willing to give up.

Follow us on our short, imaginary Ironman journey

You are surrounded by other athletes on the bank of a lake, the atmosphere is tense yet calm, and there are only a few minutes to go before the start. Thoughts are swirling around your head: "Have I trained hard enough?" "Will I make it to the finish?" "How will the swimming, cycling and running go?" But then your train of thought is interrupted by the starting signal and you and your fellow athletes rush into the water. You dive into the water, then come back up to the surface and try to get some air, which is quite hard in the first few yards. You fight for space, get jostled a little but gradually find your swimming rhythm. After a few minutes, you feel better and can maintain your speed. Now and again you try to catch or overtake the leader, and soon notice that the first discipline of the Ironman 70.3 is nearly over. You can already hear the cheers of the spectators in the transition zone; you climb quite happily out of the water and are relieved to have the swimming section under your belt.

You run into the transition zone, fetch your bike bag and get changed in the transition tent. Full of motivation, you grab your bike, push it out of the transition zone and the race now continues on land. As you start, your legs feel a little tired, but gradually you get into your stride and take over other triathletes here and there. You don't forget to eat and drink and feel that today your body is capable of great things. You occasionally have phases of fatigue and wonder if you will be able to cover the whole 56 miles. But it's ok, these moments soon pass and your legs soon feel fresh again. Now the second discipline is ending, and in the last few miles, you are relaxed as you approach the next transition zone.

In this transition zone, you put on your running clothes and then the final discipline is soon under way. Now it is hard, because over the first few miles your legs feel "rubbery" and heavy; you have the feeling that you can't run properly. But your muscles adjust because you have already practiced the transition from bike to running in training a few times. Now in the race, your legs remember how to run again. The spectators cheer you on here and there and carry you toward the finish. You don't give up when moments of fatigue occur. If you really can't run any more, you walk for a while, and are usually able to start running again after a while.

You get nearer and nearer to the finish, the crowd drives you on, you know that you can do it. Only a few more yards, then you cross the finish line. The feeling is indescribable, you want to "hug the world," all the effort and minor ailments are forgotten. You've done it. A wave of happiness flows over you; you smile from ear to ear and are absolutely elated to have accomplished your goal.

Would you like to have this feeling too?

In this book, we provide tips and tricks that will enable you to become a happy and successful Ironman 70.3 finisher.

2.1 Ironman 70.3 facts

The term "Ironman 70.3" refers to half of the 140.6-mile Ironman distance. It involves 1.2 miles swimming, 56 miles cycling and 13.1 miles of running. These course lengths are similar to the now very popular medium distance triathlon.

Since 2006, athletes worldwide have been able to participate in qualification races that lead to the Ironman 70.3 World Championships that is held in Clearwater Beach, Florida.

Check out these sites for more information:

www.Ironmanlive.com/events
www.Ironman.com

Clearwater Beach is located on the west coast of Florida. In summer, it is a popular vacation destination; miles of beaches invite you to relax and sunbathe. There are also many bridges that connect the islands and must be crossed several times during the competition. In November, it is rather quiet, but the temperature is usually still above the 90° F mark.

M. Nüsken

The inaugural World Championships event took place on November 11, in Clearwater Beach. The future of the Ironman 70.3 should be exciting, as 1,700 athletes qualified for the World Championships in the first year. In the U.S., there are eight qualifying races, which the event organizers have given fanciful names like Ironman 70.3 Timberman in New Hampshire, or Ironman 70.3 Steelhead in Michigan. Other qualifying races are being organized in Canada and Mexico, while in South America there is the Ironman 70.3 Brazil, and in Asia the Ironman 70.3 Singapore.

This 70.3-mile course is mainly of interest to and recommended for newcomers to the Ironman 140.6. The jump from the Olympic distance (1,5/40/10 km) to the Ironman distance (2.4 miles/112 miles/26.2 miles) would otherwise be too great. Some use the Ironman 70.3 as a warm-up competition before attempting an Ironman.

As for the men's and women's winning times, the women's winning times in the Ironman 70.3 are usually 87-90% of the men's. Elite athletes' winning times are, depending on the type of course, usually well below four hours.

2.2 Four reasons to do the Ironman 70.3

There are four good reasons why so many triathletes attempt the Ironman 70.3 or the medium distance:

1. **Exciting** for those who are entering new territory with the 1.2-mile swim, 56-mile bike ride and 13.1 mile run and setting themselves new and higher goals for themselves.

2. **Stimulating** for those who enjoy a race that lasts 4-6 hours and would like to explore their performance limits in this area.

3. **Interesting** for those who use the 70.3-mile race to test their mettle before the 140.6-mile Ironman.

4. **Challenging** for those who have already finished several full Ironman races but now want a highly competitive race over a shorter distance.

J. Bollwein

3 The "Four" Disciplines of the Ironman 70.3

Twenty years ago, when Henry was first preparing for the long distance, he found it helpful to compare the triathlon to a restaurant menu. This idea was his key to the mental preparation necessary to complete an Ironman 70.3 successfully.

This thought will also help you to overcome your fear before an Ironman 70.3. Imagine a menu full of everything that you particularly like to eat, and like this lavish meal, the Ironman 70.3 is a special occasion.

Our Ironman 70.3 menu:

Appetizer	Swim
Intermediate course	first transition
Main course	Bike
Intermediate course	second transition
Dessert	Run

As the first discipline, the 1.2-mile swim is considered the "appetizer." After this warm-up follows the "main course," the 56-mile bike ride. Our "dessert," which we save until last, is the 13.1-mile run. Both transitions constitute the "intermediate courses": the first from swim to bike and the second from bike to run.

3.1 Swimming: the appetizer

Swimming represents the biggest problem for many athletes, as a good technique is necessary to attain reasonable results. At the elite level, good swimming technique is the basic pre-requisite to keep up with the pace. In a race, it is not unusual to see women getting out of the water in front of or at the same time as the fastest men.

The effect of water on the body is different then that of air. When moving through cold water, the blood flows more strongly through the working musculature, which increases heat loss. In the case of swimmers who have low body fat, their body temperature is constantly decreasing, unlike their more corpulent competitors. This can be counteracted, particularly over longer distances, by wearing a Neoprene wetsuit.

For many triathletes, swimming is an unpopular or boring discipline. Athletes who really have a problem with swimming therefore usually prefer the duathlon, which consists of running, cycling, then running again. Advanced swim training is intended both to improve the swimming performance and also to make it easier to cope with the cycling part of the triathlon.

Front crawl is the fastest swimming stroke and, compared to the breaststroke, puts less strain on the legs, which will have to work hard in the second and third disciplines, cycling and running. It is therefore very challenging for many athletes to not just swim along using the breaststroke technique but to keep up with the crawlers. Anyone who is considering an Ironman 70.3 should most definitely learn the front crawl in order, as mentioned above, to spare their legs for the cycling and running to come.

3.2 Cycling: the main course

Roelie

Cycling is the second discipline in the triathlon and as the main course, it accounts for the largest portion of the whole race. In general, it is prohibited to draft other cyclists, apart from a few exceptions in the case of elite or young athletes, particularly over the Olympic distance.

Prerequisites for good performances on the bike are an optimal cycling technique and a correct sitting position, which will allow you to run with as little pain as possible afterwards. The "lying" position over the aero handlebars should not hinder breathing or the efficiency of the leg power. Many triathletes adopt the preferred "American position" on the bike, i.e. the tip of the saddle is situated well in front of the bottom bracket.

In cycling, the gluteal muscles support most of the bodyweight, which means that there is little stress on the musculoskeletal system. Even in the case of out-of-saddle riding (riding standing up), the orthopedic load is much lower than when running. In order to avoid general injuries, it is advisable to wear a helmet (a MUST in the triathlon). A helmet should always be worn, whether you are just testing a bike or popping down the road to the store.

Regardless of which triathlon distance you are aiming to compete in, the cycling component is always the longest part of the race. In the Ironman 70.3, the 56-mile bike ride accounts for the majority (50-55%) of the whole competition time. You should therefore incorporate cycling into your daily routine whenever you can.

3.3 Running: the dessert

Running constitutes the triathlon "dessert." This discipline is the most taxing for the musculoskeletal system; swimming and cycling are much less stressful for the body. Running most quickly reveals weaknesses in the core trunk musculature, the strengthening of which should not be neglected in training. Only with a strong core will your body be able to accomplish optimal running performances.

C. Micheii

As well as strengthening the core trunk muscles, your running time can also be improved with running drills. These exercises give the body a complex workout. In the "bum flick," from a relaxed trot, the heels are brought up to the glutes.

In the "knee lift," the front leg is bent at the hip and the knee is raised. The support leg is kept straight and the arms work vigorously. Running backward and to the side is also recommended. Leg crossovers involve twisting the hip and upper body in opposite directions.

For some triathletes, running in an Ironman 70.3 turns into a kind of torture. The legs are tired and heavy and the small of the back often hurts, too. It is therefore no disgrace to take a few walking breaks, soon after which it is usually possible to run again.

3.4 The transitions: the intermediate courses

The change from swimming to cycling and then from cycling to running are the "intermediate courses" on the triathlon menu. They constitute a smaller part of the whole race time. In triathlon circles, the transition is referred to as the "fourth discipline."

Anyone who is competing over the sprint or Olympic distance and wants to keep up with the front-runners should practice the transition separately. This involves taking off the wetsuit as fast as possible and then switching to the bike. Calf muscle cramps can occur when removing the swimming suit.

A particularly fast transition can be ensured by having the cycling shoes already fitted to the bike. As soon as the triathlete runs out of the transition zone, and then gets on the bike, he slips his feet into the shoes while riding. However, most athletes put their shoes on inside the transition zone, which takes a little longer. As for the transition from cycling to running, this should be practiced in training by means of the back-to-back training known as a "brick." This involves doing a running workout straight after a bike one. This "brick" training enables the muscles to get accustomed to the different loading forms. In cycling, the legs have to work with the hips tilted, but when running, the hips are extended, or upright.

ironman.com Photos

4 How to Ensure Success

**Whatever you do, don't give up;
believe in yourself and in the strength that lies within you!
NOTHING IS IMPOSSIBLE!**

4.1 Project Ironman 70.3: visions and dreams

We have slightly modified French author Antoine de Saint-Exupéry's quote, which refers to the building of a boat and the longing for the open sea:

"If you want to finish an Ironman 70.3, don't put fast athletes and training scientists together, but concentrate on the desire to reach the finish line."

Do you have dreams, but you just can't imagine yourself finishing an Ironman 70.3? The best way to start is by completing the course in your head. Marlies can still remember very clearly the time she first heard about the triathlon distances. At the time she thought: "How can I do these one after the other? Just one of those disciplines is enough as it is." Then she read in Henry's triathlon training book about a three-stage strategy, which helped her to dare taking on a triathlon.

Here is a brief summary of the three stages:

First stage: Vision, dream, challenge
Second stage: Realistic goal setting
Third stage: Execution, finish

These three stages enabled her to cross every hurdle. She was able to implement these strategies very successfully in sport and also in her professional and private life.

4.2 Systematic training leads to success

Endurance sports, and the triathlon in particular, require foresight and patience. It is not possible to enjoy a successful, long-term triathlon career without sound planning. If you are interested in exploring your performance limits, you should know that in endurance sports, nothing can be achieved in the short term, but only in the medium and long term.

At least 5-6 years of training are required. This is true for everyone, regardless of age or gender.

However, if your training is monotonous and the intensity and content do not change for months or even years, then you should not be surprised if your performances do not improve.

One reader asked Henry: "I have been doing triathlon for five years, over Everyman and short and medium distances. Throughout this period, my performances have stayed the same though. I would really like to improve, what do I have to do to get faster?"

The answer, in brief, was: Have a look at the overall structure of your training in your training diary. You should start with the way the whole year is structured and end with the weekly training plan. I am sure that your training is

1. very monotonous and
2. has no periodization.

If you divide your training year into periods with different training intensities and content, your performances are bound to improve. A systematic yearly structure contains three different long periods.

4.3 Training periods

- Preparation
- Competition
- Transition

The periods are different for novice triathletes than ambitious and performance-oriented athletes.

4.3.1 Monthly organization of training

Beginners and senior triathletes (over the age of 40) should organize their training year as follows:

Preparation phase:	February-May	four months
Competition phase:	June-September	four months
Transition phase:	October-January	four months

For ambitious and elite triathletes:

Preparation phase:	January-May	five months
Competition phase:	June-October	five months
Transition phase:	November-December	two months

If your motivation is dwindling, which can easily happen with a long-term competition program spanning several years, it is advisable to incorporate an active rest year. During this time, you should not enter any particular competitions; just do light, relaxed workouts without any competitive aspirations. Many athletes do this in the last year in their age group in order to enter the new age group with renewed enthusiasm. If two partners are very committed to the triathlon, it is possible to alternate every year.

4.3.2 Preparation period

After an active rest phase, most triathletes are glad to return to organized training. The first two months of this phase serve to build basic endurance. This is the basis for the occasionally more intensive training in the second phase. The volume is systematically increased from low to medium loading intensity. Adequate recovery and regeneration should not be neglected. The main training method is the *endurance method*.

Cross-country skiing and cycling on stationary rollers and other endurance sports all improve basic endurance. General conditioning can also be improved by strength endurance training during these months.

W. Freidl

Who is block training for?

Block training is recommended during the preparation phase for triathletes with limited time available for training and those who cannot do cycling training during the whole year due to weather conditions. This **block training** extends over a period of four weeks and can work like this:

January	swimming
February	running
March	cycling

The running and swimming months can also be swapped. What this actually means in practice is that during the **swimming month**, swimming training is increased and running training is reduced. Increased swimming training can mean *doubling your training*. If you normally practice swimming once a week, double this to twice. If you normally train twice a week, double it to four times. If the weather is suitable, now is the time to start your first bike rides.

During the **running month**, running training is increased and swimming and cycling training are reduced. Increased training can mean doubling your training. If you usually run twice a week, *double* it to four times a week. Please be careful not to increase your running training too suddenly, but do so gradually. If your basic training consists of running 20 miles per week, then you should gradually increase it as follows:

25 miles, 30 miles, 35 miles, 40 miles then back down to 20 miles again. If you run three times per week, you should increase to five times per week. If the weather permits, go cycling too.

During the **cycling month**, cycling is increased and swimming and running training are reduced. If you are able to organize a one- or two-week training vacation with your family that emphasizes cycling, this emphasis should also be adequately prepared in training. Otherwise, days off should be used for the organization of the cycling month. If you manage a few gentle bike rides a week for a whole month, you will have a good base for the whole triathlon season.

Just a small observation beforehand about **training your weakest discipline**: The ideal time to work on this is during the preparation phase. There is just one snag though. This is usually the discipline you enjoy least. There is a simple way to get around this:

Make sure you train for your weakest discipline in an appropriate group. This makes it easier to overcome any unwillingness to train, as group training is more motivating, and the relaxed banter will help you get over your lack of enthusiasm. As soon as you have reached a certain standard in your weakest discipline, you may really start to enjoy it.

To have the greatest prospects of success, practice your weakest discipline at least 3 times a week. The second stage of the preparation phase (6-8 weeks) is characterized by a reduction in volume and a moderate increase in intensity. Fartlek running training or the occasional fun run can be added to spice up training. In cycling, carry out a few time trials cycling between signs or markers, such as those that note city limits.

Brick training, especially the bike-run combination, can be added to the training program in April.

Bike-run brick training
Short, sharp bike session, e.g., 40-45 minutes + longer, more relaxed run 70-80 mins
Longer, more relaxed bike session, e.g., 90 minutes + shorter, sharper run over 20-30 mins

Under no circumstances should you forget the regeneration week after three training weeks.

Ambitious athletes should do over-distance, low intensity training once a week throughout the preparation phase. This is not appropriate for beginners, as we are talking about running or cycling for several hours. This is intended to improve the fat burning (60-70%) that is so important for endurance athletes. One way this can be achieved is by running for 2 hours or cycling for 3 hours at a relaxed pace (T2-T3).

4.3.3 Competition period

No triathlete can be in peak form for the whole four or five months. It is therefore advisable to aim to peak two or, at most, three times. The first section of this phase is the time for warm-up competitions. These enable us not only to test form but also to try out equipment, different tactics and refreshment strategies. Between the first test triathlons you should still train at a fast pace, apart from the last three days before the race. Normal training sessions alternate with regeneration weeks. Make sure you get enough rest after every competition, which is determined by the length of the triathlon, your fitness level and age.

Very fit athletes regenerate faster than others. The competition intensity is also a factor. If this was only 90% instead of the usual 100%, then the regeneration phase will be shorter. It will take a triathlete with very good endurance a week to recover from a short triathlon, while beginners may need two weeks. Thereafter, normal training can be resumed. After an Ironman 70.3, 2-3 weeks recovery should be taken. Obviously, no other competitions should be entered during this period.

Triathletes with many years of experience may also tend to break this rule, if they don't intend to give 100% in the next triathlon. The number of competitions per year is determined first by the course length and then by fitness, age and attitude. By attitude, I mean:

There are a number of triathletes who are completely relaxed about competing in triathlons and enjoy them. They just like measuring themselves against others in fair rivalry, not fighting with them. They fight against the length of the course, not the other competitors! Other athletes, on the other hand, are a little obsessive and believe that the triathlon is the be-all and end-all and put themselves under great psychological pressure. They completely forget that our sport should be fun and that there are other things in life apart from swimming, cycling and running.

4.3.4 Transition period: the time for regeneration

The last peak performance of the season is over. Now it is time for everyone to take a deep breath and even to take a whole week off, without feeling guilty, before looking forward to the next training month.

In this phase, avoid silly ideas, like running a marathon. This will work for a year or two, but then the body will react to the inadequate regeneration with illness or injury. The triathlete quite simply needs a long regeneration phase at the end of a strenuous season. Now you have the time to practice other pursuits that you didn't have time for during the rest of a year.

These pursuits should include interpersonal relationships, i.e. spending more time with friends, acquaintances and, of course, your own family.

During this time, your aim should be to recover physically and psychologically in order to gain new strength and motivation for the coming season. The importance of motivation is very often underestimated. Someone who is not motivated cannot perform to the best of his ability. Motivation is one of the prerequisites for being a successful triathlete, as it creates the willingness for systematic training.

Training during this phase should be relaxed and playful and the volume should be minimal. A few excess pounds are the external sign of a good recovery phase for many triathletes. The copious food intake of the preparation phase should be reduced, as the daily nutrition requirement is now greatly reduced.

And don't forget the all-important review of the whole season. Ask yourself: Did I get the preparation right? Did I peak at the right time? Did my triathlon results do me justice? Did I get the training volume and intensity right? Did I manage to balance my work, home and sport, etc.? All these questions need to be answered self-critically.

Don't forget the all-important question: Did I reach an acceptable balance between effort and reward?

In order to remember your hopefully honest answers to these questions, they should be written down in your training log. Don't answer the above questions without using your daily training log.

4.4 Three essential training principles

1. Increase training load

Significant performance improvements can be achieved by dividing the training year into phases of differing loads and intensity. Several systems in our bodies react to loads with a corresponding adaptation. This is a protection mechanism on the part of the body to ensure that it will not be overwhelmed by another similar load.

2. Training: from general to specific

Training at the start of the triathlon year should prepare the athlete's system, such as the cardiovascular system, and the general athleticism for the loads to come. This does not necessarily need to involve swimming, cycling and running but could take place on the cross-country skiing course, speed skating rink or in the gym. That means that as far as strength endurance is concerned, general endurance and strength should be trained separately. Special strength endurance can be trained later in the preparation phase.

3.   Alternate training and recovery

Regeneration time after training is just as important as the training itself. During training, catabolic and anabolic processes take place in our bodies. When we feel good, it means they are in balance. If we start to draw on our performance reserves during intensive or long-lasting training, our performance ability declines. We feel tired. After the load, the body enters the regeneration phase. Our body not only returns to its previous level but it lays down additional performance reserves for a possible future load, if we allow it sufficient time to do so. This is called **supercompensation,** and means that a performance improvement does not take place during an arduous 90-mile bike ride but afterward in the recovery phase. However, if the body is not given enough time to recover, instead of increasing, the performance level drops.

It is therefore essential to allow our bodies to go through these recovery phases if we want our performances to improve! This applies to a weekly cycle, a monthly cycle and particularly an annual cycle. There will be more detail on this in the section on specific training plans.

4.5 Planning the triathlon year

The transition phase and long winter evenings lend themselves well to the planning of the coming triathlon year. This is a time to dream of the great event, of the unforgettable run to the finish, of great success, of qualifying competitions, winning one's age group, etc. And rightly so! This is how we motivate ourselves again to enjoy the long bike rides with our training friends, swimming in the lake and relaxed runs.

When planning we should never lose touch with reality. Very few triathletes are able to train for 20-25 hours per week or attend a one- or two-week training camp. However, it is also possible to succeed with much less training and the right attitude.

So back to our planning: We should be wary of the opinion that there is only one training plan or one path to success. Fortunately this is not true, for many roads lead to Rome. We certainly do not need to become training slaves in order to enjoy the diversity of our sport and the excitement of competing in the long term.

Performance enhancement not only requires the planning and execution of training but also the correction of our mistakes. If a training mistake is acknowledged as soon as possible, and a change is made immediately, nothing is lost, but stubbornly repeating mistakes means that the seasons' goals will not be met.

A well-designed training plan must be drawn up anew every year.

The following three periods should be incorporated into the training plan:

• the new training year

• the previous training year

• long-term development

A phase of continuous, moderate load-increase is more likely to lead to the desired performance improvement than an excessive increase in the total annual training load. Continuous load increases should not exceed 10%. Beginners may even double their total training load in the following year.

You should proceed as follows when establishing your annual training plan:

a) "Current state"
Take stock of your current performance ability. Ambitious triathletes have a thorough knowledge of the performance data relating to their state of fitness. This is hard for beginners to ascertain, as they do not yet have any competition results available.

b) Realistic goal-setting
In simple terms, you cannot plan without a goal and cannot have a goal without planning.

However, someone who just wants to be fit and healthy and has no desire to achieve a special performance goal during the year can always just do the same old training, although this monotonous training will get boring.

c) Plan your competitions
The Ironman 70.3 calendar is determined about 10 months in advance. Make sure you know how to enter these competitions and always apply early. Several events book very, very quickly. In the case of the big one, the Ironman, the 2,000-plus available places are often taken within a matter of hours. You can find out more about this on the Internet at: www.ironmanlive.com

d) Divide the year into training phases
A systematic annual plan consists of three phases of differing lengths. These several-month periods are further divided into 4-6 week stages. The weekly or monthly swim, bike or running training volume can already be set in the annual planning. The detailed planning of individual training sessions takes place just before the start of the phase.

e) Detailed planning of the 4-6 week stages
In the last step the individual training sessions for each stage are planned. In regions in which it is possible to cycle year-round, this can be incorporated year-round into the training plan.

f) Holistic approach to training planning
Setting up a training plan does not just involve working towards a certain goal (e.g. the Ironman 70.3 in 5 hours) and doing whatever it takes to achieve this. What use is the greatest triathlon result if my family, or my

private or professional life suffer in the process? Unfortunately, we all know people who have made this mistake.

Our solution:
All sporting activity should be geared towards developing an all-round healthy athlete. Someone who has a *third life* alongside his professional and private life, (i.e., his life as an athlete). The athlete's whole environment must be taken into account in planning and implementing training for this to be accomplished successfully.

4.6 Your environment

Amateur triathletes have to coordinate three significant factors into their lives: their professional lives, their private/family lives and the sport of triathlon. This is not always easy, particularly when intensive preparation for an important event, like an Ironman 70.3, is involved. As well as planning and good organization, there is one crucial factor that is easily forgotten, which we shall call "environment."

Environment is the compilation and balance of an athlete's life and its parameters. Here are the most important parameters (building blocks) represented in the illustration below:

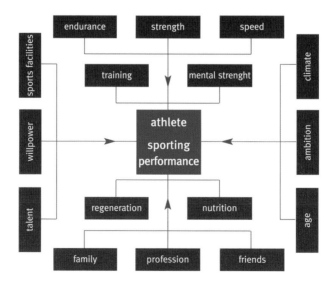

Fig. 1: The individual environment of the triathlete.

If you take a look at each parameter and compare yours with those of other triathletes, you may have better circumstances than your fellow athletes, possibly even better than your current training partner who has just become the father of twins and is also in the process of building his own house. Or the mother of five who works and is nevertheless preparing for an Ironman 70.3. You will say, that's impossible; it just can't be done. But Michaela and her husband from Austria showed us that it can be done. A few years ago, both successfully finished an Ironman and their five children aged between 3 and 24 are justifiably proud of their parents.

Forty-six year-old Peter, who recently become enthusiastic about triathlon after more than 20 years as a strength athlete and has a physically taxing job in mechanical engineering, is another example of the diverse background triathletes comprise. All of these factors make it all the more gratifying that he is a regularly successful Ironman 70.3 finisher.

According to Henry, we can be **successful** if we manage to observe three basic principles:

- enjoy training

- integrate the sport into our professional and private lives

- prepare sensibly for competitions

It is important for all of us take our individual capabilities and our strengths and weaknesses into account in the yearly planning stage. The more performance-enhancing parameters (building blocks) that we manage to include, the better our performances will be. Our training suggestions are only intended to be recommendations that you should adapt according to your capabilities. As a constructively critical athlete, it is up to you to decide, as we do not know your individual circumstances. Only a personal coach who knows your individual environment and your capabilities can give you precise training guidance. We're sure that you'll be able to transfer the important basic principles and training tips that are relevant to your individual circumstances.

Along with our training recommendations, we also present practical training examples and personal information about the triathletes concerned to illustrate some possible training solutions.

4.7 Heart rate

Skinfit

The existence of pulse monitors, or more accurately, heart rate monitors, means that it is no longer necessary to depend on subjective feelings for training feedback because these devices reveal exactly how hard we are training. Despite their undisputed usefulness, we should not forget to listen to our bodies though, and always take into account how we feel when determining the right training load. It could be that after a hard day's training we are simply exhausted the next day and therefore cannot drive our heart rate high enough. Instead of worrying about it, we should listen to our body and reduce the training intensity.

The heart rate monitor gives us important information about our current training load. Again, that does not mean that we only train with the heart rate monitor. In the short-term, it helps us develop a feel for a certain load. Before we discuss a few figures and percentages for correct training, here is a list of factors that can influence heart rate:

Influences that **raise** the heart rate are:
Heat, altitude training, stress, residual alcohol

Influences that **lower** the heart rate are:
Cold, rain

Influences that can **raise or lower** the heart rate are:
Fatigue, medication, air pressure

Obviously, we cannot always train exactly according to predetermined heart rates. They are benchmark data and auxiliary quantities, whose effect we should neither overestimate nor underestimate.

So, take both body awareness and heart rate (HR) into account in training and competition!

Performance diagnostics are an accurate way of determining target heart rates for the different training areas. These performance tests involve measuring blood lactate levels. Numerous institutes, sports physicians and gyms offer these tests. As there are several different ways of scoring these tests, bear in mind the following when it comes to performance diagnosis:

- Choose an experienced institute where you can build up a relationship over the years.
- It is usually not possible to compare data obtained from different institutes.
- Make sure that you always take the tests under the same conditions.
- Make sure you are given a thorough explanation of how to transfer the results into everyday training.
- Competition results take precedence over performance diagnosis tests.

Performance enhancement is achieved by setting the right stimulus at the right time. The load level is determined by the rhythm of our hearts. As there are plenty of references in the literature to heart-rate percentages, we will refer to the simplest value, the **maximal heart rate**.

Athletes' heart rates can vary as much as their shoe sizes. Even in the case of identical performances by different athletes, their heart rates are different. Heart rates largely depend upon the following factors:

- Age (the maximal heart rate falls about one beat per year)
- Genetic disposition
- Fitness level
- Gender (women have values of 8-10 beats higher than men at the same load-intensity).

How do we determine our maximal heart rate when running, cycling and swimming?

A few facts about the resting heart rate

When the heart rate is measured in a state of rest, it is called the **resting heart rate**. This value depends on the person's training condition and is fairly constant. A very low resting heart rate does not automatically mean greater performance ability. In order to maintain good reference values, the resting heart rate should be taken lying down first thing in the morning. The measurement of the resting heart rate is important for several reasons:

- A slowly and regularly increasing pulse at the start of the year indicates improved training condition.

- A value that is raised by 8-10 beats per minute indicates health problems. This is either a sign of overtraining or is the first sign of an infection. There is a particularly high danger of this during or after training camps.

- If you have a raised resting heart rate, you should immediately reduce your training and just do regenerative training or avoid training altogether.

Maximal Heart Rate
Our highest heart rate (HRmax) depends on our genes, training condition, age and gender. As a rough benchmark, this can be calculated by the formula: 220 minus age (for men) and 226 minus age (for women).

How to measure the HRmax
The precondition for self-measurement of the HRmax is an immaculate state of health. Failing this, the measurement should only be carried out under medical supervision, e.g. in the form of an exercise ECG.

The simplest way to measure this value is using the now common waterproof heart rate monitor. As the HRmax varies during running, cycling and swimming due to the different muscle proportions involved, the HRmax measurement should be taken during each discipline.

HRmax – swimming
After a warm-up 500m swim, a 200-400m long sprint produces the highest heart rates in the water. This value can be 10-15 beats per minute lower than when running.

HRmax – cycling

After a half hour warm-up, interspersed with short sprinting bursts, run a 2-2.5 mile stretch flat out on level terrain, or uphill if you have access to a long enough climb. The distance to be covered depends on the gradient. The cycling HRmax is usually around 5-10 beats per minute less than when running.

HRmax – running

To obtain a HRmax when running, warm up for 15-20 minutes, then sprint for 1,000-2,000 yards. A very accurate method for competitive athletes is to take the HRmax during the final sprint of a 5,000m race.

Table 1: Our training levels T1-T8

Tempo-level	% of HRmax	Type	Description and Application
T1	65	Very gentle	Regeneration training and long to very long sessions. Difficult to maintain due to the constant sensation that you could be running faster.
T2	70	Gentle	Basic training to improve fat metabolism; training between hard training days.
T3	75	Relaxed	Establishing the base, long sessions, should be able to talk easily, as in T2, main training zone for the cardiovascular system. Stimulation of mitochondria – our energy system.
T4	80	Quick	Tempo work starts here; for longer fartlek and tempo runs and bike rides.
T5	85	Fast	Training in the anaerobic threshold zone, use is regulated. Limit loads in the first two months of the preparation period.
T6	90	Hard	Approaching race pace for the Ironman 70.3. In training, improving basic speed.
T7	95	Very hard	Totally unsuitable for beginners, improvement in the anaerobic zone, in intervals only in the short-term. Training for sprints and short distances.
T8	100	Maximal	Competition tempo in solo competition 3.1-mile run or 12.4-mile cycle or 550-yard swim.

Your personal heart rate

		Swim (e.g., 185)	Run (e.g., 190)	Bike (e.g., 200)
My maximal heart rate	% of HRmax	Date	Date	Date
T1	65			
T2	70			
T3	75			
T4	80			
T5	85			
T6	90			
T7	95			
T8	100			

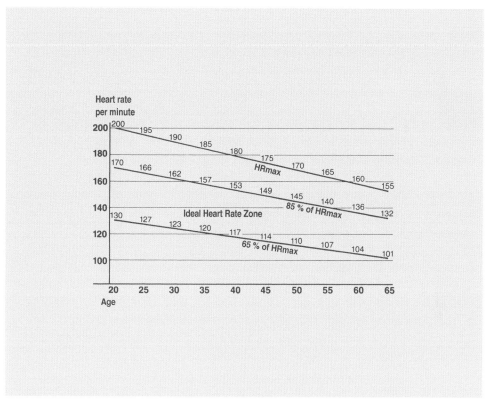

Fig. 2: The ideal heart rate (rough guidelines).

4.7.1 Threshold training

To start, the limit training load for beginners should be T5 or 85% HRmax. Two factors are important here: aerobic and anaerobic processes.

Aerobic metabolic processes require oxygen for the supply of energy in the body.

Anaerobic metabolic processes do not require oxygen to provide energy. The intensity of the training load determines which is used in training. The threshold between them is blurred and there is no definite boundary.

Training at the boundary of aerobic and anaerobic energy supply is often called **threshold training**. Exact heart rates for these thresholds can be determined in performance diagnostics tests by checking lactate levels and heart rates.

As a rough guideline, below 85% of HRmax energy is provided aerobically. Above 85%, the process is predominantly anaerobic, causing the build-up of lactate (lactic acid), which greatly diminishes athletic performance. This gives us a severe burning sensation in our leg muscles. The fitter an athlete is, the better the metabolic processes function in his body.

Tempo levels T1-T4 correspond to the aerobic zone, while the fast and intensive tempo levels T6-T8 correspond to the anaerobic zones. Threshold training therefore involves our tempo levels T5/T6.

Ambitious and performance-oriented triathletes should train more frequently in these zones than beginners because this type of training pushes the threshold zone higher. However, this does not mean that these athletes should always train in this zone. Over the medium term this would be excessive and lead to overtraining.

Experienced triathletes can get a good feel for this threshold by warming up, then training for 45 minutes flat out on the bike or on foot. The loading heart rate measured here is around the anaerobic threshold, and it should be different for cycling and running.

In any case, after an anaerobic workout in zones T6 and T7, you should perform an aerobic workout on the following day.

4.7.2 General training structure

Triathlon training is advanced endurance training. If you try to make up for missed training with a four or six week crash course, or only perform intensive workouts in this time, illness and injury will most certainly result. What is required is systematic, regular, long-term training in order to ensure short-term and long-term success. We have already mentioned the 5-7 year period required to reach our performance peak, if that is what we want. We say "want" quite deliberately, as nobody is forced to find out their performance limits, but many triathletes find this a fascinating journey.

If you work constantly toward your goal, you will achieve it.
Even the longest journey starts with a single step!

The great thing about endurance events is that we can allow ourselves time to achieve our goals. We do not need to have accomplished everything by the age of 35 as perhaps soccer players do; we can give ourselves time even into our 40s, 50s, 60s and 70s.

- The primary training commandment (principle) should be:

Training is not a competition!

Training represents preparation for a competition. If you turn every workout into a competition, you will never achieve your full potential in competition because your body will never be allowed to recover sufficiently. As already mentioned, training and recovery go together. There is often the danger of training too fast in groups where a few members want to stand out and show what they can do and how good they are. These "Training World Champions" tend not to do as well as they could in competition, as they are burned out due to training too hard.

In general, group training is a great thing. It is fun and makes even long or intensive workouts seem easier. We should bear the goal of every workout in mind.

- Training should be practice for competition.

- A competition gives us the possibility to demonstrate our athletic ability – not against, but with others.

You should begin every workout with a gentle 10-minute warm-up, followed by your training program, which in turn is followed by a gentle (cool-down) phase. Finish with a few all-important stretching exercises.

Further stretching and strengthening exercises can be carried out twice a week in front of the TV in the evening.

For the purposes of training planning, we differentiate between **core** and **peripheral training**.

Core training refers to long or intensive workouts, while **peripheral training** refers to the relaxed, gentle training and the all-important training-free recovery stage between the core training stages.

- **Core training is normally supported/paired with peripheral training.**

Core and peripheral training therefore belong together; they form a whole and only together do they lead to training and competition success.

4.8 Core and peripheral training

Core Training + Peripheral Training = Total Training

"Core training" consists mainly of the substantial workouts in terms of both volume and intensity. "Peripheral training" complements core training.

Fig. 3: Core and peripheral training.

4.8.1 Distribution of training volume

For the following training plans, we roughly follow this distribution of training volume in four weekly training rhythms:

Week 1	Week 2	Week 3	Week 4
Normal week	Normal+ week	Hard week	Regeneration week

Fig. 4: Distribution of training volume.

e.g.

Week 1	Week 2	Week 3	Week 4	Average
8 h	8.8 h	9.6 h	4.8 h	7.8 h
6 h	6.6 h	7.2 h	3.6 h	5.8 h

In our suggested training programs below, we usually go from the second training week (normal+) of every separate training month. That means that for the first training week we reduce the suggested plan by around 10%, for the third week we increase by 10%. For the fourth week, we halve the training of the third week.

4.8.2 Training intensities

We have used the following terms and abbreviations for the different training intensities:

HRmax Percentages	Training level terms	Training level abbreviations
100	Competition pace 3.1 mile run, 12.4 mile bike, 550 yard swim	T8
95	Very hard training	T7
90	Hard training	T6
85	Very quick, fast training	T5
80	Quick training	T4
75	Relaxed training	T3
70	Gentle training	T2
65	Very gentle training Regeneration training	T1

Fig. 5: Training intensities and corresponding abbreviations.

There are many different ways of categorizing types of endurance training, e.g., basic endurance training, which is further divided into easy and moderate, etc. To simplify matters, we use the abbreviations T1-T8 (T = tempo, with the levels 1-8).

4.8.3 Training loads

Personal triathlon performance enhancement is critically dependent on the athlete managing to find the right balance between loading and regeneration. Important factors in monitoring this are:

- How you feel while training
- Heart rate and possible data from the performance diagnostics
- Overall sense of well-being

To avoid the danger of over-training, an important tip:

- If the fatigue is in your muscles, then just train gently or relaxed;
- If the fatigue is in your mind, then don't train at all!

By 'fatigue in the mind' we mean that you don't feel like training or lack motivation!

The exact distribution of training levels depends on the training period and the triathlete's own ability. This can be found in the training plans in chapters 6, 7 and 8.

In general, the distribution of training intensities in the **competition period** looks like this:

Training levels	Ironman 70.3 Beginner	Ironman 70.3 Ambitious	Ironman 70.3 Performance Oriented
T1 Reg.	15%	10%	5%
T2			
T3	80%	70%	70%
T4			
T5			
T6	5%	20%	20%
T7			
T8			5%

Fig. 6: Distribution of training intensities in the competition period.

For example, the ambitious athlete Gudrun trains 10 hours per week in the competition period. She should train for 1 hour in T1, 7 hours in T2-5 and 2 hours in T6-T7. Note that the training emphasis is always predominantly in the basic endurance zone T2-T5.

4.9 Regeneration and supercompensation

Triathletes often neglect regeneration, but it is an essential part of training. These regeneration measures and rest periods allow our performances to improve. It really is true that "strength is in stillness." Muscle development takes place when our body is regenerating and resting. Also the tendons and ligaments used during training need a "vacation" from time to time.

Some active regeneration options are a very relaxed bike ride, relaxed swimming without pressure, or just going for a stroll. Passive regeneration measures include sleeping (very important), massage, alternate hot and cold showers, sauna, etc.

Our bodies have the gift of being able to regenerate in **excess** of the required amount, and in this way we are equipped to deal with new, higher loads. It thinks that if today I ran 8 miles, the day after tomorrow I might have to be able to run 10 miles. This ability is called supercompensation, and without this effect, performance enhancement would be impossible. Supercompensation only works if there is sufficient regeneration. So, for example, if training is gradually increased over a three-week period, the fourth week is regeneration week, to enable the body to recover, after which the body is given new training stimuli. However, if the new training stimuli come too soon, then the body is unable to adapt and performance levels stagnate or even drop. In the worst case, this leads to overtraining, and the body requires longer rests in order to recover. If you are quickly exhausted, nervous and unmotivated, suffer from flu or a virus then you should not train at all. Otherwise you risk inflaming the cardiac muscle, which would endanger your health. You can read more about the subject of *overtraining* in the book *The Complete Guide to Triathlon Training,* chapters 9-10.

4.10 Increased strength and flexibility

Written in collaboration with physiotherapist and psychologist Carmen Himmerich

Strengthening
Triathletes do need muscles, but too much muscle is a hindrance in endurance sports, such as the Ironman 70.3, where the muscle mass must be carried for 70.3 miles. Therefore a lot of thought must be given to how muscle mass is to be developed.

In swimming, strength can be developed using paddles; in cycling, by riding up steep hills; and in running, by doing hill runs and short stretches.

Strengthening exercises enable us to gain additional strength and compensate for the normal muscle atrophy that occurs after the age of 40. At the same time, blood flow and metabolism in the musculature improve. We can perform strengthening exercises both in the gym, on the various machines and equipment or at home using our own bodyweight, in which we take advantage of the lever effect of the extremities and gravity.

Endurance sports already strengthen a large part of our musculature. However, there are muscle groups that are barely used during training, like our core muscles (the trunk). Strong core muscles are not only important in the water in order to maintain a stable position, but also during the second discipline, the cycling. A strong core is necessary in order to remain injury-free. Without compensation exercises, several hours of cycling and running can have a negative effect on the spine and lead to pain and unpleasant tension in the musculature.

On the next page are some of the most important core muscle strengthening exercises.

A few brief tips for the **correct execution** of the **strengthening exercises**:

1. Always perform all exercises on both sides of the body.

2. Breathe calmly and quite normally; don't hold your breath.

3. Duration 15-30 seconds, 3-10 reps, rest 30 seconds.

Strengthening Exercises

1. Oblique abs

Starting position: Lie on the back, raise the head and place hands relaxed around the head.

Execution: Move the elbows and knees, while keeping the other leg in the air; change to the other direction.

Possible errors: Performing the exercise too fast and hyperextending the lumbar spine.

2. Abs

Starting position: Lie on the back, raise the head and hold your arms by your side.

Execution: Alternately bend and straighten the legs, keeping head and arms in the same position.

Possible errors: Performing the exercise too fast and hyperextending the lumbar spine.

3. Back and gluteal muscles

Starting position: Lie on your stomach with your arms stretched in front of you.

Execution: Raise the head and one arm off the floor while also raising the opposite leg. The body should keep the raised extremities apart. Keep the head in line with the spine, look at the floor.

Possible errors: If you look ahead, your spine will hyperextend.

4. Trunk and gluteal muscles

Starting position: The forearms are placed on the floor so that the elbows are situated below the shoulders.

Execution: The body is raised in a straight line. Hold this position and raise one leg.

Possible errors: The abs should be tensed so that the lumbar spine does not sag.

5. Lateral trunk

Starting position: Lie on the side with one forearm on the floor.

Execution: Raise the hips from the floor so that the whole body forms a line. Hold this position for 40-50 seconds.

Possible errors: Tilting the pelvis forward or backward.

Stretching

Unfortunately, stretching exercises tend to be neglected by triathletes, but the consequences of not stretching will be felt after a while. As the muscles are regularly strengthened and therefore tensed during swimming, cycling and running training, it is imperative that they are returned to their original length at the end of a workout. If this is not done, the result can be muscle shortening, hardening of the muscles and tendon insertions and thus movement limitations. These limitations have different effects. For example, if the hip muscles are not stretched, an athlete's running stride becomes shorter. In the case of shortened chest and arm musculature, it is more difficult for the triathlete to extend the arms far forward when swimming.

An additional advantage is that stretching also improves the body's blood circulation, promotes regeneration and improves coordination. A "cold" muscle should not be stretched, as it is too vulnerable to injury.

The best time to stretch is after training and/or after the strengthening exercises mentioned above, but not before or directly after an intensive workout or competition.

A short guide to the **correct execution**:
- Always carry out all exercises on both sides of the body.
- Breathe calmly and completely normally when stretching. Don't hold your breath.
- Stretching duration after training: 15-30 seconds, repetitions 2-4, rest every 30 seconds.
- Pulling is allowed, pain is to be avoided.
- Stretch slowly and keep the muscles still (no bouncing or rocking).
- As a rule, stretch after the workout.
- However, after an intensive workout or competition, you should wait an hour before stretching.
- The higher your training volume, the more intensively you should stretch.

As all the stretching exercises are shown in detail on pages 271-280 in the book *The Complete Guide to Triathlon Training*, we limited ourselves to just listing suitable exercises to avoid repetition in this book.

Stretching exercises
- **Lateral neck musculature**
- Triceps and muscles of the upper back
- Chest muscles
- Lateral trunk musculature
- Front shoulder muscles, chest muscles and the inner upper arm

- **Cycling and running**
- Long and short calf musculature
- Thigh musculature
- Hip flexor musculature
- Inner thigh musculature (adductors)
- Hamstrings
- Gluteal musculature and mobilization of the spine
- Chest musculature and the lateral trunk musculature

4.11 Triathlons in hot weather

In this chapter, you will start to sweat! Medium distance and Ironman 70.3 competitions usually take place in latitudes in the summer where temperatures around 86°F and above are common. Warm weather is also not rare at the Ironman 70.3 World Championships in Clearwater Beach, Florida, despite it being held in November.

It takes the body about a week to adapt to heat stress. Sweating increases and adapting to heat entails the body's core temperature dropping about 1°F in the heat center of the brain. The lower body core temperature makes the heat center of the brain react more sensitively to higher outside temperatures. The temperature difference between body core and external temperature allows sweat to flow sooner, and the sooner you start to sweat, the sooner your body cools.

In high temperatures, your pace should definitely decrease to avoid the risk of long-term health damage. If possible, you should train in the morning, late afternoon or the evening. You should avoid training at midday as the sun is at its hottest.

If your core body temperature rises above 104°F, your health is in danger. Inadequate fluid intake stimulates a rise in the core body temperature. Even if you are not thirsty, you must drink constantly otherwise your heart rate will increase. Don't just drink water though; add sodium to the water, otherwise you may suffer from "water poisoning," which occurs when sodium needed for water absorption in the stomach is removed from the blood. Concentration imbalances can occur, and in the worst case, too much water without electrolytes can lead to edemas in the lungs or in the brain.

In competition, the heat is not such a big problem while swimming and cycling, especially cycling, as additional cooling is provided by air circulation. However, while running, it will be immediately obvious whether sufficient liquids have been drunk during the race. Take advantage of every aid station during the 13.1 miles, and use the sponges offered to you to cool your head.

Some potential heat-related ailments

Heat collapse
Symptoms are paleness and problems with balance. If you feel these symptoms, lie in the shade, raise your legs, cool your head and take sips of liquid.

Heat exhaustion
Excessive sweating (cold sweat), headache, and possibly fatigue, disorientation and marked drop in performance. Relief can be obtained by lying down and trying to get cooled off. Medical assistance should be sought and a salt solution consumed if necessary.

Heat stroke
This is the most serious form of heat-related illness, characterized by motor skills disturbance and disorientation (the skin also feels warm and dry). In the worst cases, collapse and loss of consciousness can occur, in which case the only solution is an immediate trip to the hospital in order to obtain medical assistance.

4.12 Triathlons in cold weather

You should not be afraid of freezing during a triathlon, as summers at the locations of competitions are not usually freezing cold.

However, there are also cooler periods e.g. in Europe, in which case the cold can easily become a problem for the Ironman 70.3. The danger in training in low temperatures is that the muscles will become too cool, to the point that the body temperature is too low to keep the body warm. If we also take into account the wind chill factor, things can get really serious, particularly when cycling, when performance levels can drop considerably. While swimming, you are protected by your Neoprene suit and swim cap (or even two). If you then jump onto your bike with a wet suit and dash off you should not be surprised if you get sick after the race. Marlies and Henry have gotten into the habit of equipping themselves with dry clothing in cold temperatures, as cold muscles do not work as well as warm ones. These few extra seconds in the transition zone can easily be made up in the rest of the race.

K. Käfer

Wind chill

If the weather is both cold and windy during the cycling element of the triathlon, be extra careful! The "wind chill" factor is the difference between the measured air temperature and the perceived temperature. It is totally feasible that even in the summer, the temperature during a triathlon is only 50°F. At a cycling speed of 20 mph, the temperature felt by our skin is only 34°F. The skin temperature of triathlon pros, who can reach speeds of 30 mph, can drop to 30°F.

It is obvious that in these circumstances good performances are no longer possible. The cooling effect of the headwind should also be taken into account. The muscles cool, the body temperature drops and good performances are impossible.

H. Ash

5 Ironman 70.3 Equipment

We could discuss the subject of equipment for hours, but in order to keep within the scope of this book, we will limit ourselves to giving you a few tips regarding the purchase of equipment. Triathletes can usually be distinguished from runners or cyclists by their striking and colorful outfits, and their equally futuristic bikes. A certain passion for detail is an indisputable characteristic of the triathlete. Marlies rides a pink bike because "she is a girl" and loves the color pink.

5.1 Swimming

Neoprene
The main function of the Neoprene wetsuit is to prevent the body from getting cold during long swims. In competitions, the water temperature determines whether the competitors wear Neoprene wetsuits or not. These suits cover the whole body (although there are models that do not cover the arms) and are closed at the back by means of a zipper.

There are many different models, and the fit should be good, slightly tight but not overly so, so that air can still get in. It is extremely important to have freedom of movement in the shoulder area. Ideally you should try the suit in water before purchasing it (many stores already offer this service). Weaker swimmers benefit more from the improved buoyancy than good swimmers.

Swimming goggles

Never swim without swimming goggles! It is almost impossible to orient yourself without goggles when swimming. The swimming goggles should be watertight and not fog up. You will need to try out different swimming goggles to ensure that these conditions are met.

Find swimming goggles that suit you by trial and error!

Goggles that fit well will adhere to your face even without the rubber straps. You need to be able to see properly in order to orient yourself and enjoy swimming. The coating on the inside of the glasses is quite sensitive, so you should never rub the goggles with a rough towel. In order to prevent them from fogging up, you can find sprays on the market. A simpler and cheaper method is to put a little saliva on the inside of the goggles, quickly rinse the goggles in water and then put them on.

Swim cap

Thin bathing caps are usually provided for the competitors, which must be worn. In an Ironman 70.3, it is usually a good idea to wear another swimming cap underneath this one due to heat loss. A few athletes also wear two caps to make their goggles fit better and ensure they don't come off, especially at the start of the race and when swimming around buoys.

One-pieces and swimming trunks

In an Ironman 70.3, ambitious and performance-oriented triathletes pull on a one-piece underneath the Neoprene suit so they do not waste too much time in the transition zone. Beginners and less ambitious triathletes wear swimming trunks or a swim suit under the Neoprene suit and during the transition take the time to get changed for cycling. Particularly in cold weather, we prefer to change completely, as cold muscles cannot perform well. "Lost time" is easily made up, as you will not spend the first miles on the bike shivering with cold.

5.2 Biking

Racing bike

The majority of the Ironman 70.3 is spent on your racing bike. It is therefore crucial to find the optimal sitting position so that you can get through the competition relatively comfortably.

Our motto is: Go for it and enjoy yourself!

It will take a while to find your ideal position. After a few years of triathlon, your cellar will probably contain a few stems, handlebar extensions and saddle posts that you needed to try out. It is important that you (and not other people) feel comfortable on your bike during long rides and do not have to shift around in the saddle because the position is wrong.

M. Nüsken

Clip pedals

We recommend clip pedals for a better transmission of force. Getting into and out of them requires a little practice to start with; Marlies initially fell over with the bike a few times at an intersection, because she had not yet mastered the lateral turning out movement of the foot.

Aero handlebars

If you use aero handlebars – and you should do so for the Ironman 70.3 – then your bike will be very aerodynamic. The arm and shoulder muscles used during swimming will be offloaded and the aero handlebars allow for a relaxed upper body posture. In addition, the use of aero handle-bars takes the pressure off the upper body in preparation for the final run.

Helmet

Please, please, please: Always use a helmet when cycling, even just for a quick ride into town or when trying out a new bike. Accidents happen easily. It may not even be your fault; all it takes is for another driver not to see you. You should therefore protect your head. We are also role models for children and young people. Marlies knows from her own experience that wearing a helmet can prevent serious injuries. In one race, she slid on a wet curve in the road and her helmet broke, but it protected her from a serious head injury. Whether the helmet is broken or not, it must always be replaced as soon as possible after a fall. Today, helmets are well-ventilated and also protect the head from the sun. More and more athletes in races are wearing aero helmets. These look cool and also bring time advantages at high speeds and in long races.

Saddle

Manufacturers produce different saddles for men and women, and you should also try these before you buy them. If you are constantly slipping back and forth after a few miles during long races, you should probably try another model. Some stores allow you to test saddles to make it easier for you to find the right one for you.

Cycling shoes

The cycling shoes should fit. Even with bare feet they should not cause pressure marks or chafing. As well as being well-finished on the interior, Velcro™ fastening should allow you to take them on and off quickly. When you buy them, make sure that you can also run a little in the shoes, so that you don't trip over or fall in the transition zone. In short triathlons, most athletes do not wear socks to save time. For an Ironman 70.3, however, you should take the time and put on socks straight after the swimming as this makes cycling more comfortable and avoids the formation of blisters during the subsequent running. Pros and performance-oriented athletes have their cycling shoes mounted on their pedals because every second counts.

Clothing

Cycle tights have padding that protects your rear from pressure marks. After the first long cycle workouts in spring, your bottom will be slightly painful. This will fade after a few rides as your body gets accustomed to the activity. Relatively tight cycling jerseys are suitable for training, as this makes them as aerodynamic as possible. In the back pocket of the jersey keep a snack, money and your cell phone.

5.3 Running

For the final discipline – the running – running shoes are the most important piece of equipment. There is no such thing as the perfect running shoe for everyone, so you have to find the one that best suits you. The best idea is to go to a specialist running store where you can get accurate advice. When purchasing shoes, you should take your time and go to the store in the afternoon, as at this time your feet are slightly swollen and somewhat larger than in the morning. It is advantageous to take your old running shoes with you so that the sales advisor can see from the way the sole has worn away to determine how you position your feet when you run. Many stores offer a foot position analysis, so bear this in mind as it will make it easier for you to choose the right shoes. Purchase stable shoes for training and a slightly lighter pair for racing. This lighter pair should also be worn for faster workouts.

Quick-fastening straps

To not waste unnecessary time in the transition zone undoing laces, we recommend quick fastenings on running shoes. These fastenings are mounted on the laces – with one flip they are closed and you can start running immediately. At the tips of the laces, you should tie a knot so the quick fastener does not fall off the laces when you take the shoes off.

Our tip:
Put some glue in the knots so that they don't come undone.

Socks or support hose

Socks are THE link between the foot and the shoe. Functional socks made of microfiber prevent the formation of blisters. If you wear cotton socks, you shouldn't be surprised if they cause chafing or blisters. Especially for running, socks are very important; when running 13.1 miles, it is worth putting on socks in the transition zone. Even the pros take the time to put socks on, as painful blood blisters can cost a victory. Henry is one of those triathletes who wears knee-length compression socks for a better running feeling and thinks that this is worth the inconvenience of putting them on in the transition zone.

Clothing

Cotton vests are not optimal for running as they get wet quickly and dry slowly. All-in-one triathlon suits or microfiber running-tights and jersey are more suitable, as they have a moisture-wicking effect. A cap will protect you from the sun. Some caps have a headband inside that absorbs sweat to stop it from running into your eyes.

L. Bänziger

T. Frahm

6 Training to Finish the Ironman 70.3 (6:00 hours or more)

"If you want to build a high tower, you must take your time building the foundations."

(Anton Bruckner)

If your goal is to be an Ironman 70.3 finisher, you will need perseverance and endurance. You need a solid training foundation to be able to cope with a medium distance triathlon.

6.1 The last six months before the race

This chapter deals with training for triathletes who have set themselves the goal of finishing the Ironman 70.3 around 6 hours. This includes countless beginners, but also those with a limited endurance background who want to finish the 70.3 miles. In this training group, the aim is definitely "just" to finish. There is extensive training advice for more ambitious and performance-oriented triathletes in chapter 7.

Although the competition will last 5-6 or even 7 hours for novice and less ambitious athletes, those with a good endurance training base cope significantly better with the distance of 70.3 miles than a standard marathon of 26.2 miles. Nobody with a good endurance training base should be afraid that after the competition they will have no challenges left.

Prerequisites for successfully completing this 70.3-mile competition course are:
- At least one year of regular endurance training
- Participation in one or more half-marathon races
- Bike rides for 3 hours
- Endurance swims of 30-50 minutes

Anyone who is in this position six months before the start has the best prospects of success.

How much training will I need in order to complete an Ironman 70.3?
Beginners should work out around 7 hours per week in the last two months before a competition.

Here, this simple formula applies:
Your weekly training volume should be the same as your competition finish time, i.e., at least 1.2 miles swimming, 56 miles cycling and 13.1 miles running.

There are surely athletes who can manage on less training, while others may need more. This is determined by the athlete's overall environment (as discussed in Ch. 4.6).

Approximate required competition times for the 6-6:30 hour target

	Target: 6-6:30 hours
Swimming 1.2 miles	about 45 mins
Cycling 56 miles	about 3 hours 10 mins
Running 13.1 miles	about 2 hours 10 mins
Transition times	about 10 mins

Figure 7: Competition times for a 6-hour Ironman 70.3.

The following training suggestions are derived from the above-mentioned target times:

View these amounts, intensities and days of the week as recommendations. We don't know your individual possibilities and also cannot predict the weather conditions.

Your eagerness to train should be tempered by four things:

- Always feel comfortable!

- Be partner-friendly in training!

- Don't forget your post-workout stretch!

- Distribute workouts and 1-2 rest days evenly throughout the week!

For example: Two days training (Tuesday, Wednesday), one day rest (Thursday), three days training (Friday, Saturday, Sunday) and another rest day (Monday). Performance-oriented athletes are also allowed one rest-day per week. Novices and masters (above the age of 40) should usually still have two rest-days per week though. Masters athletes, who are in their 50s, should schedule their regeneration week after two training weeks.

Therefore, the goal is to master the 70.3-mile triathlon distance in about 6 months or 26 weeks!

The first Ironman 70.3 competitions usually take place at the beginning of June. Therefore start your training month in December.

6.1.1 Training month 1

In December, your new life begins! Always keeping in mind the great and inspiring Ironman 70.3 goal, look for other comrades-in-arms with whom to work on basic endurance in the gray winter months. Jogging for 45 or even 60 minutes, the first swimming sessions in the indoor pool, but also mountain bike rides, cross-country skiing, exercise bike riding at home or Spinning® workouts at the gym serve to improve our general endurance.

It is particularly advisable to improve your swimming technique. Taking front crawl lessons or hiring a good swim teacher will pay off. Adapt your training to the weather conditions and motivate members of your family, your friends, neighbors or work colleagues to do an occasional workout with you. The rest days offer several alternatives to eating plentifully.

You should already be working out three times a week. Keep a training diary.

6.1.2 Training month 2

The training diary rejoices with every addition. It may help to make every 15 minute activity a training point.

4 x 4 = 16 training points should soon be possible. A New Year's Eve race can be an inspirational goal. Run for fun, without any pressure, 2-3 times per week. Don't forget to stretch after running. If you enjoy going to the gym, you should do so. Use light weights and high numbers of reps. Cross-country skiing is another way of improving basic endurance. Varied and long-lasting exercise is the key to success. The training tempo is moderate (60-75% of HRmax is sufficient). An initial two-week swimming block can be carried out.

6.1.3 Training month 3

A. Lenft

After three normal training weeks, the fourth week should be a regeneration week in which your training is now reduced by 40%. For swimming, you should use longer intervals. 5-6 x 200m, 10 x 100m and technique drills will ensure progression. A two-week running block is recommended. You could finish off with a 10k, 15k or half marathon race. If the weather is good, now is the time for the racing bike or mountain bike to come into its own. 20 training points (five training hours) are a great weekly target in this period.

Training months 4, 5 and 6 (14 weeks) are presented on the following pages. Please, please, please: Don't adopt suggestions without testing them. Don't stick rigidly to the plan. Bear in mind your own capabilities and the recommendations in chapter 4.

6.1.4 Training month 4

Training week 1, about 6-7 training hours (week: normal)
- Tues.: Swim 1 mile, warm up/down, 3 x 400 yds endurance method T3
- Wed.: Run 1hr 15 mins fartlek
- Fri.: Swim 1 mile, warm up/down, technique exercises + intervals 4 x 200 yds.
- Sat.: Run 1hr 50-2 hr, gentle tempo, 70%, T2
- Sun.: Bike ride if weather is good, or 1hr gentle (75%, T3) run or cross-country skiing

Training week 2, about 7 hours (week: normal+)
- Tues.: Swim, 1-1.2 miles, with intervals 110/200/300/200/100 yards, T4
- Wed.: Cycling, 1hr + running, 1hr 15 with fartlek
- Fri.: Swim, 1-1hr 10 miles endurance method, warm up/down. 2 x 500 yds, T3
- Sat/Sun.: Run, 1hr 50-2hr, gentle tempo, T2, 70%
- Sun/Sat.: Bike-ride over 2hr, relaxed with 90 rpm pedaling

Training week 3, about 8 hours (week: hard)
Running week:
- Tues.: Swim, 1-1.2 miles with intervals, T3/T4 + 1hr gentle run, T2
- Wed.: Run, 1hr 15 fartlek
- Fri.: Run, 1hr 15 relaxed T3
- Sat.: Cycling, 2-2.5 hr, pedaling gently, 90 rpm, T2
- Sun.: Run, 1hr 40, with 2 x 20 min tempo endurance runs (85-90%, T5)

Training week 4, regeneration week, 4-5 hours
4 x relaxed, T3, one-hour activities as desired, one of which should be a run.
If you take long bike rides on the weekend, you will improve your basic endurance with a gentle endurance ride.

Training week 5, about 7 hours
Focus: Swimming
- Tues.: Swimming, 1.5 miles, technique + intervals 100/200/300/400/300/200/100 yards, T5
- Wed.: Running, 1hr 15 fartlek
- Fri.: Swimming, 1 mile, warm up/down, technique exercises + intervals 4 x 200 yds, T4
- Sat.: Swimming, 1.25 miles, warm up/down, 3 x 400 yards endurance method, T3
- Sun.: Bike-ride, 2-2.5hr, relaxed with 90-100 rpm, T2-T3

6.1.5 Training month 5

In training month 5, the focus is now on additional form enhancement with the aim of finishing an Ironman 70.3 or a medium distance triathlon.

During this period, go on the longer bike rides that are now necessary to create and improve basic endurance. It is important to ride at a relaxed tempo, with about 90-100 rpm. That is not easy for a novice cyclist, but they should at least try to stick to these values. Our knee and leg muscles will thank us later!

When you first practice the transition between cycling and running, in the first two miles of running you may feel as though you will never be able to run 13.1 miles. Don't worry though; after practicing the bike run transition a few times, your running will improve and your muscles will get used to this unfamiliar change of activities. Do not be discouraged if you have to walk a short distance. In general, you should try to run very gently after the transition. In a few weeks, try a "brick" workout consisting of very gentle cycling followed by a quick 30-40 minute run.

As before, swimming training consists of intervals – the shorter they are, the faster they should be performed, with 20-30 second rests – and endurance swimming. Endurance sessions of 3-4 x 500 yards are quite sufficient for the purposes of training swimming endurance. If you feel that you ought to perform long 1.5 mile swims, you may do this once every 2-3 weeks. The advantage of the shorter endurance sessions is that during the rests (about 30-40 seconds), we can improve our swimming technique. At the same time, ask others for help, perhaps a training partner or an experienced swimmer can check your swimming style. Just a little tip regarding correcting your swimming style: Don't try to work on 4-5 corrections at the same time, but work on one point at a time.

Training week 6: cycling week (about 12 hours)

- Tues.: Running, 1hr 30, relaxed, T3
- Wed.: Cycling, 2hr, with quick bursts (5 x 10min), up to T5
- Fri.: Cycling, 2-3hr, relaxed, T3, + 50 min endurance swimming, T1-T2
- Sat.: Cycling, 2-3hr, gentle ride, T2, + 50 min fartlek run, T3-T5
- Sun.: Long, gentle bike ride, 3-4hr T3.

Training week 7: about 11 hours

- Mon.: Cycling, 2-3hr, with 5 x 10min tempo, T6-T7, + 30 min relaxed pedaling
- Wed.: Swimming, 1.25 miles with intervals, T3-T5
- Fri.: Swimming, 1.5 miles, warm-up/down, 4 x 500 yds, T3-T4
- Sat.: Cycling, 3hr, T3 + 50 min. running, T3
- Sun.: Bike ride over 2-3hr, T3, with 90-100 rpm

Training week 8: regeneration week, 5-6 hours

4 x one hour of gentle exercise of choice, one of which must be an hour's running.

On the weekend, a long, gentle bike ride at 100 rpm to further improve basic endurance.

Training week 9: about 8 hours

- Tues.: Swimming, 1-1.25 miles with intervals, T3-T5, + 1hr running, T2
- Wed.: Cycling, 1-2hr with a little fartlek
- Fri.: Running, 1:15hr, T3
- Sat.: Cycling, longer ride 3-4hr, relaxed pedaling, T3, 100rpm
- Sun.: Running, 1:40hr, with 2 x 20 min tempo endurance run, T5, relaxed swimming, T3

Training week 10: about 9 hours

- Tues.: Swimming, 1-1.25 miles, with intervals, T3-T6, + 1hr running, T2
- Wed.: Cycling, 2hr, T2, with 2X 30min, T5
- Fri.: Running, 1hr 30m T3
- Sat.: Cycling, longer ride 3-4hr, pedal relaxed, T3, 100 rpm
- Sun.: Running, 1hr 40, with 2 x 20 min tempo endurance run, T5, relaxed swimming, T3

A few general comments:

Adapt the suggested training to your individual capabilities.
Don't let training become a chore. You should enjoy it!

- It is better to drop a training session rather than do it badly.

- Occasionally train with a suitable partner.

- Be partner-friendly in training.

- When in doubt, always aim your training toward the improvement of basic endurance.

- Basic endurance forms the foundation for an Ironman 70.3 or a medium distance triathlon, which is why if you are in doubt you should always gear your training toward improving basic endurance, i.e., with a clear emphasis on a training intensity between 65-80/85% of HRmax (T2-T5).

- Athletes in their 50s should schedule a week's regeneration training after every two weeks' training. For those in their 40s, the frequency of the regeneration week is dependent upon their training condition.

If you will already be taking part in your first triathlon at the beginning of May – in which case the swimming usually takes place in an open air pool – you can incorporate this into your overall training.

These triathlons usually involve the Everyman or Olympic distance. As well as the normal exertion of a competition, they can also be used to improve speed and test out equipment.

On the day before the competition, you can safely drop your normal training. Enjoy the first test of the season. If you like running and would like to take part in a half-marathon in April, this can also form part of your training. I would only recommend a full marathon for very committed and experienced runners, as they are better able to run in a deliberately controlled way than novices. Otherwise, there are plenty of low-key endurance competitions that can be entered by athletes who enjoy competition. Use this welcome change to focus on the main goal, which is the Ironman 70.3. Don't forget the all-important post-race regeneration though.

6.1.6 Training month 6

While the first part of our training was dedicated to basic training, and the second part to form enhancement, the third part is all about the all-important fine-tuning for the grand finale, the big day.

At least one short triathlon should be scheduled before the first Ironman 70.3 or a medium distance triathlon. This can be done on full training, and serves as a genuine test of both form and equipment.

If the competition takes place in open water (lake), a Neoprene wetsuit is a great help. You should train in the Neoprene wetsuit a few times beforehand. Even though it makes it easier to swim, you should still look for landmarks when swimming in natural surroundings. It is of course possible to swim without a Neoprene suit, and one may also swim breaststroke for the whole 1.2 miles. In Hawaii, in 1985, admittedly one of very few, Henry swam breaststroke, and he climbed out of the water after 1hr 34 mins (2.4 miles). During the cycling and running, there is still enough time to make up for lost ground.

During the longer bike rides, you should nibble an energy bar and drink regularly. Only use in competition what you have tested during training.

Should the triathlon take place on a Saturday, then do not train at all on Friday. You could also stop training two days before a competition.

If you are in similar shape – as re-presented below – and training for your first Ironman 70.3, you can go to the starting line with a clear conscience. Of course, you have not trained hard enough to hope to win, but the main point is that it should be fun. The goal you have set for yourself is finishing, not winning.

Being successful means finishing! Or in other words: You don't have to win to be successful.

Finishing means reaching the finish line after swimming for 1.2 miles, cycling for 56 miles and running for 13.1 miles. It means rising to the self-imposed challenge of swimming, cycling and running for 70.3 miles using the power of your own muscles.

A worthwhile goal!

If you would like to invest more time in training, you can do so. In this case, you should particularly heed the general training principles, i.e., pay attention to regeneration weeks, tempo change, maintaining basic endurance training and a sensible diet.

In the last week before the medium distance triathlon, you should train so little that you feel guilty. All you really need are a couple of relaxed sessions.

Your training plan can (not must) look like this in the last four weeks:

Training week 11: about 11 hours

- Tues.: Swimming, 1.25 miles, with intervals, T2-T5
- Wed.:   Cycling, 2-3 hours, T3, with 5x10 min tempo, T6, + 30 min run, T2
- Fri.:   Swimming, 1.5 miles, warm up/down 4 x 500 yds, T5
- Sat.:   Cycling, 3 hours, T3, +50 min running, T3
- Sun.:   Cycle ride over 2 hours, T3, 90-100 rpm.

Training week 12: regeneration week, about 5-6 hours

4 x 1 hours' relaxed exercise of choice, one hour of which should be a running workout.

On the weekend, a long, gentle cycle ride at 100 rpm to further improve basic endurance. 1 x bike-run "brick" (transition workout)

Training week 13: about 10 hours

- Tues.: Swimming, 1-1.25 miles, with intervals + 1 hour running, T2
- Wed.:   Cycling, 2 hours, with a little fartlek
- Fri.:   Running, 1hr 15, T3
- Sat.:   Cycling, long ride 3-4 hours, T3, 100 rpm + 30 min run, T3
- Sun.:   Running, 1hr 40, with 2 x 20 min tempo endurance run, T5-T6, relaxed swimming

Training week 14: competition week

- Tues.: Swimming, 1 mile endurance swimming, T3
- Wed.:   Cycling, 1 hour, T2, with 2 x 10 min quick bursts, T4
- Fri.:   Running, 30-40 min quite gentle, T1
- Sat.:   Check your bike, pack, traveling if necessary
- IRONMAN 70.3 1.2/56/13.1 miles – FINISH!

What follows are two regeneration weeks, which you should spend practicing your favorite sports quite gently (60-65%).

A second competition of a similar length is possible in August, or the beginning of September, to wind up the season. Before then, you will have the time and opportunity for a few shorter distances.

6.2 A Practical training example

How such training recommendations can be converted into reality, or not, is shown by the example of the Swiss athlete Dan B., who started systematic endurance training exactly one year before his Ironman 70.3 in Switzerland and went on to finish it in an astonishingly relaxed way in only 5:50 hrs.

Here is Dan's story:

Dan is in good physical condition at age 46, 5'7" tall, 136lb. Prior to the year before his Ironman 70.3, he had only done occasional mountain bike rides, only swam breaststroke and when he occasionally ran, he had knee problems.

First training steps one year before the Ironman 70.3:

- Treadmill analysis and new running shoes. Since then he has not suffered from knee problems.
- First attempt at swimming crawl in Lake Faak, Austria, with the result that after a few weeks of training, he could already crawl 110 yds in one go.
- Regular 20-35 mile mountain bike rides.
- First training on the Ironman Austria 56-mile cycling course.
- First short bike/run workout.
- Finished first Everyman triathlon 500 yards/12.5 miles/3 miles.
- Until Christmas: 2-3 x per week: 1 hr endurance swimming, learning crawl technique and 1-2 x 3-5 miles running with walking-breaks, heart rate 130-140.

Dan's training

January, February and March:
    2-3 x per week, 3-5 miles run, pulse 130-140
    3-4 x per week, 1:15 hr gentle endurance swim in crawl style

April:
    2-3 x swimming, as before
    2-3 x running, as before
    1 x cycling

The last six weeks look as follows:

4th week of April (9hr training)
Focus on: Endurance training

Date: from   to   Week:

Day	Weight lb	S Dist. yard	S Time	C Dist. miles	C Time	R Dist. mile	R time	Other sporting activity	Comments	Resting pulse rate	Weight lb
Mon.		2,200	Interv								
Tues.						6.2	52				
Wed.		2,200	end.								
Thurs.						6.2	55				
Fri.											
Sat.				31							
Sun.				45		6.2	52				
Totals:		4,400		76		18.6					

1st week of May: (3.5 hours training)
Focus: short triathlon

Date: from   to   Week:

Day	Weight lb	S Dist. yard	S Time	C Dist. miles	C Time	R Dist. mile	R time	Other sporting activity	Comments	Resting pulse rate	Weight lb
Mon.											
Tues.											
Wed.		2,200	endur								
Thurs.											
Fri.											
Sat.				31							
Sun.		900		24		5	45	Comp.	2:16 hrs		
Totals:		3,100		55		5					

2nd week of May: (10 hours training)
Focus on: endurance training

Day	Weight lb	S Dist. yard	Time	C Dist. miles	Time	R Dist. mile	time	Other sporting activity	Comments	Resting pulse rate	Weight lb
Date: from		to			Week:						
Mon.		2,200	Interv								
Tues.						6.2	51				
Wed.		2,800	Endur								
Thurs.						6.2	50				
Fri.											
Sat.				30	2						
Sun.				45	2hr 40	6.2	60		Cross training		
Totals:		5,000		75		18.6					

3rd week of May: (12 hours training)
Focus on: cycling

Day	Weight lb	S Dist. yard	Time	C Dist. miles	Time	R Dist. mile	time	Other sporting activity	Comments	Resting pulse rate	Weight lb
Date: from		to			Week:						
Mon.		2,200	Interv								
Tues.						6.2	52				
Wed.		2,800		Endur							
Thurs.								Short vacation			
Fri.				45		3.1	30		Cross training		
Sat.				30		6.2	50		Cross training		
Sun.				45							
Totals:		5,000		120		15.5					

4th Week of May: (10 hours training)
Focus on: endurance training

Day	Weight lb	S Dist. yard	Time	C Dist. miles	Time	R Dist. mile	time	Other sporting activity	Comments	Resting pulse rate	Weight lb
Date: from		to			Week:						
Mon.		2,200	Interv								
Tues.						6.2					
Wed.		2,800	Endur								
Thurs.						6.2	52				
Fri.											
Sat.				30							
Sun.				45		6.2	55		Cross training		
Totals:		5,000		75		18.6					

1st week of June: Competition week:
Focus on: Ironman 70.3 Switzerland

Date: from	to		Week:							
Day	Weight lb	S Dist. yard	Time	C Dist. miles	Time	R Dist. mile	time	Other sporting activity	Comments	Resting pulse rate	Weight lb
Mon.				45	2hr30						
Tues.											
Wed.											
Thurs.											
Fri.											
Sat.											
Sun.	Water 57° F	1,000	34	60	3hr05	13.1	2hr02	5:50 Ironman 70.3	Cycling 1,100 HM		
Totals:		1,000		105		131					

Usually in this race, the distance swum should be 1.2 miles, but because of the cold water (only 57° F), the distance was only 1 mile.

6.3 Dan: "A dream come true"

Once I had successfully completed a triathlon sprint distance following the summer vacation, it was clear to me that training would continue. Week after week, I trained for the three disciplines without motivation problems. I enjoyed exercising in the open air and the swimming pool, without being pressed for time or ambitions for elite performance. After one month, I asked myself: What is your next goal? What is the purpose of all this training? I needed a sporting goal. I toyed with the idea of the Ironman for quite a while. The "ultimate" event was still out of my league, but the Ironman 70.3 in Rapperswil, Switzerland, was an attractive goal that came just at the right time.

I wanted to be part of it. Confident in the knowledge that my mentor Henry Ash would be accompanying me, I sat in front of my computer and enrolled. Now I knew there was no turning back.

Preparation

In January, the real preparations began. I took a beginners course to improve my crawl technique. Apart from very few running drills, I was swimming up to four times a week in the pool. At the beginning of March, I was already a little faster than when swimming breaststroke. For me, as a complete swimming novice, who had mastered my first crawl strokes during summer vacation, this was the first big success. With the warmer weather, I started to go out on the bike more. The aim was to cover the half distance workout every week. Finishing the Ironman 70.3 was my main objective. My family supported me by allowing me a lot of freedom for my sporting activities.

Feelings while training

In the workouts, I had enough time to reflect on different things. My thoughts were often in Rapperswil and with my family. Then, serious work-related problems nearly threw me off track. I reached the point where I lost sight of my goal of the Ironman 70.3. Training became unsatisfying and joint pains I had never felt before made me think about abandoning my athletic ambitions. After about three weeks, I suddenly realized that if that were to happen, I would lose my coveted starting position in Rapperswil. I sat down, closed my eyes and tried to imagine myself running toward the finishing line after 70.3 miles. A feeling of warmth and relief came over me. I suddenly realized how I would accomplish the Ironman 70.3 and resolve my work-related problems. I managed to make it through my psychological low point. Thanks to my endurance training, I sorted out my problems like a true future Ironman. I now worked toward my sporting goal with renewed joy and enthusiasm. The nearer the big day came, the more joy I felt. I was glad I had not given up. And the big day came. My dream of finishing the Ironman 70.3 in Rapperswil was starting to come together.

The Big Day – Finishing the Ironman 70.3 in Rapperswil

I forgot the lows of the preparation period and quite honestly only felt butterflies in my stomach on the way to the starting line. I enjoyed the swim in the cold water of Lake Zurich, had a ball cycling the difficult 56-mile route through my Swiss home and absolutely floated toward my big goal during the half marathon. The more than 1,000 participants whom I passed several times on the turn around point, the numerous spectators and even the total of 200 steps that had to be overcome did not discourage me. When there were only 1.5 miles to go, I felt happier than I had ever felt before. Then I saw the long and so keenly awaited goal. Henry ran with me over the last few yards, and I finally enjoyed

L. Bänziger

the moment of finishing. I didn't let myself down. I am simultaneously glad, grateful and happy to have done it: The ultimate achievement of my life, to have swum, cycled and run for 70.3 miles on my own. I was able to make my sporting dreams come true in less than a year, and at the age of 46!

Today I am convinced that endurance sports give us extra reserves to cope with life's problems. I will continue the sport of triathlon with great enthusiasm in order to do something good for my body, to make my dreams come true, to build up my reserves and last but not least, to be able to enjoy these unique moments with like-minded people. Even if this particular dream ends here, I already have plans and clear goals that I would like to accomplish in the months and years to come.

I wish all athletes could have a mentor like Henry, who communicates the joy of triathlon with an exceptional understanding of both his sport and human nature.

Dan

M. Nüsken

7 Training for Ambitious and Performance-Oriented Athletes

A triathlete whose greatest stimulation is testing his personal limits is therefore more committed than triathletes who just want to finish. We call these people ambitious and performance-oriented athletes (groups A and P).

Here is just a brief reminder that our classifications should not be interpreted too rigidly.

Athletes/ Description	Approximate Goal	Competition time	Group
Beginner	To finish	6 hrs or more	B
Ambitious	To test performance limits	5:50-5 hrs	A
Performance- oriented	To test performance limits/win	4:20- 4:50 hrs	P

Figure 8: Triathlete classifications.

7.1 Training for ambitious athletes (A: 5:50-5 hrs)

In order to achieve these times in competition, specific performances are required.

7.1.1 Required race split times

Realistic Goal	5 hrs-5:50 hrs
Swimming 1.2 miles	34-40 min
Cycling 56 miles	2:35-3hr
Running 13.1 miles	1:45-2hr

Fig. 9: Individual times for a target time of 5 hrs-5:50 hrs.

If you want to do more than just finish the Ironman 70.3, or medium distance, you are already an experienced triathlete. The majority of age group athletes fall into this bracket. They usually have the advantage of having been physically active for years and therefore have good or very good basic endurance. The strengths of younger triathletes on the other hand are usually their speed endurance and speed strength. We know that endurance is easier to train than speed strength, as the tendency to possess speed strength muscle fibers is innate.

For those athletes who come by way of the Olympic distance and are tackling their new challenge, the Ironman 70.3, we usually recommend a little less emphasis on tempo training, but more on basic endurance training. Athletes who have previously preferred the Ironman distance should include more tempo work in their training, replacing a few long workouts.

7.1.2 Performance-related prerequisites

If you are ambitious about competing over the 70.3 miles, you should try to achieve the following individual performances and train systematically:

* To swim 2,200 yards in less than 42 minutes

* To cycle 25 miles in less than 1:12 hrs

* To run a 10k in less than 42 minutes

This is a base on which to build. Systematic Ironman 70.3 training starts with the training schedule. As explained in chapter 4, this covers the whole year, not just the competition season.

This book is not intended for the easily swayed mind who just wants to do an Ironman 70.3 or a medium distance of more than 60 miles for the heck of it just once, because they do not have a sound training base or will get injured. However, here is the example of Emil from Munsterland, Germany:

Emil, a wiry 35-year-old, is a spectator on the triathlon course and watches with mixed feelings as over 200 participants swim for 1.2 miles, cycle for 56 miles and then still manage to run 13.1 miles. "I could do that! I am going to do it next year! That's my thing," Emil proclaims to his companions on the course. Later, he also tells those at home.

Nine months pass without him putting these words into practice. Suddenly, Emil was reminded of his boast, and he sets to work. Well-meaning advice to prepare his debut slowly and start with shorter distances falls upon deaf ears. He rashly spends $3,000-4,000 on new triathlon equipment. "Now I can do it," he again proclaims. With great gusto he then proceeds to train like mad. He wants to show everyone he can succeed. The first injuries caused by overtraining are ignored. Triathlon, triathlon and more triathlon is his motto, as though it was the be all and end all of his life.

Our Emil actually became a finisher. He finished, but how? Instead of the planned time below 5 hours, he did it in over 7 hours. He suffered from cramps and injuries. "But I can do triathlons now, why should I still train and enter competitions," was his reaction.

The actual reason was his hasty, far too excessive and intensive training, he had "trained in" several injuries that troubled him greatly during the competition. He could not even think about actually running. Instead, he accomplished his goal limping and completely exhausted.

From then on, training and the triathlon were history to him, which was a shame, as he was physically very well-suited for triathlon.

Later he confessed he was both mentally and physically completely burned out (after training for only 3 months).

So, remember to train in a way that provides – conditioned by a good basic endurance – a stable foundation for all your athletic endeavors.

Bear in mind, every triathlete has to take his or her individual surroundings into account when planning and later executing the training if he or she wants both fun and success in this sport.

Detailed information for improving swimming, cycling and running performances can be found in chapter 8.

7.1.3 Annual structure

Transition Time: October, November, possibly December and January. 2 x weekly relaxed jogging, 1-1:15 hr, if possible light bike ride, 2 x weekly swimming training with emphasis on technique improvement. In the winter, the focus is on analyzing of the previous season and planning the coming one.

Preparation Period: January, February (first part), March, April (second part)

Competition Period: May to September, possible start of November World Ironman 70.3 Championship in Florida.

7.1.4 The last six months

As far as training volume is concerned, we structure our training rhythm in a 3:1 ratio, i.e., three weeks loading with a 10% increase every week. The fourth week must be for regeneration.

We structure the load days per week in a similar way:

For seven days: Two days loading, one day regeneration, three days loading, one day regeneration.

A regeneration day can also mean 1 hr relaxed endurance swimming or a gentle bike ride of 20 miles for well-trained endurance athletes.

So:
* Week 1: Normal week with 1.0 training ratio.
* Week 2: Normal+ week with 1.1 training ration, i.e. week 1 +10%.
* Week 3: Hard week with 1.2 training ratio, i.e. week 2 + 10%.
* Week 4: Regeneration week with 0.6 training ratio, i.e. exactly half of the hard week, dropping all intensive workouts.

www.sailfish.com

Masters (above age 40), who are approaching 50, should drop the hard week. They train predominantly in a 2:1 ratio, i.e., two load weeks, one regeneration week, or two load days, one regeneration day, two loading days, one regeneration day + one day of complete rest. Absolute rest means no exercise at all.

January:

The first part of the preparation period. Training volume increases with low physical load, with a heart rate of 130. Blood circulation is stimulated by stretching and light strengthening exercises. Overall, the aim is to build and improve general basic endurance, for which a variety of exercise types should be practiced.

1 x weekly long, gentle run over 13 miles, or if you want to run an early marathon, 18 miles. Occasionally participate in causal runs, but without running flat out.

If the weather is good on the weekend, go on a 1 hour relaxed bike ride. If you enjoy Spinning™, or exercise bike training, this is a good way to prepare for cycling training. Swimming: 2-3 x per week, technique training, endurance swimming and short intervals.

If you would like to **focus on swimming**, go swimming as often as possible this month. If you live near a pool or can go at lunchtime, you will be able to do it more often than someone who has to travel far. It would be ideal to swim 2,000-2,800 yards 3-4 x per week. 1 x endurance swimming, e.g., 2 x 1,000 yards or 4 x 500 yards. Otherwise, do interval swimming lengths, e.g., 2 x 6 x 100 yards, 2 x 4 x 300 yards, with one minute rest, pyramid swimming, 1, 2, 3, 4, 5, 6, 7, 8, 7, 6, 5, 4, 3, 2, 1 lengths.

Day	Training	Comments
Mon.	–	Stretching, sauna
Tues.	50 min. run	Running, T3
Wed.	60 min. swim	Technique exercises, intervals, 4 x 100 yds, 4 x 200 yds, T5-T7, **core training**
Thur.	75 min. run	1,2,3,4,5 min. fartlek, up to T5
Fri.	–	
Sat.	60-90 min. cycling	Gentle, T2, alternatively 120 min cross country skiing
	60 min. swimming	Endurance, warm up/down, 4 x 500 yds core training
Sun.	20km running	Relaxed, T3, stretching, **core training**
	Total: about 8 hours	

Fig. 10: Recommended training for training week 2 in January, "Normal+ week" without focus on swimming.

Reduce training for week 1 by about 10%, and increase by about 10% for week 3. Week 4 then becomes our regeneration week, when we halve the training in week 3 and only train relaxed, i.e., T3.

February:
We continue our training to build and improve general basic endurance during this month. From now on, any form of exercise is welcomed.

If you have not yet gotten your mountain bike or racing bike out of the garage, as soon as the weather permits you should do so and go for your first bike rides.

If you would like to run a half or even a full marathon in the spring, you should focus on running now and add an extra running session. For more details, see "Running Training" in chapter 8. The beginning of March would be a good time for a brisk half marathon, followed by a regeneration week.

Day	Training	Comments
Mon.	–	Stretching, sauna
Tues.	60 min. run	Running, T3
Wed.	30 min. exercise bike	
	60 min. swimming	Technique exercises, intervals, 8 x 200 yards, T5-T7, core training
Thur.	75 min. run	1,2,3,4,5 min. fartlek, T5
Fri.	–	
Sat.	60-90 min. cycling	Gentle, T2, alternatively 120 min cross country skiing
	60 min. swimming	Endurance, warm up/down, 4 x 500 m core training
Sun.	12-13 miles running	Relaxed, T3, stretching, core training
	Total: about 8-9 hrs	

Fig. 11: Suggested training for training week 2 "normal" in February.

For weeks 1, 3 and 4, see January's guidelines.

March: Focus on cycling
During the Ironman 70.3, we spend about 50-55% of the competition time on the bike, so we should structure our training in a similar way. This means making up for the previous months, but by a balanced distribution of training, not by going flat out.

In March – depending on the weather conditions – sometimes even in the first half of March, the all-important cycling endurance training begins.

This should be the focus on the weekends. Rides of 40- 50 miles or even 60 miles at 90-100 rpm in a low gear are important. For example, you could ride Fridays 30 miles, Saturdays 45 miles, Sundays again 30-35 miles, and possibly Wednesdays 25 miles. The aim here is to improve

basic cycling endur-ance, for which relaxed pedaling is required. We can then confidently drop the third running unit per week.

The best plan would be to go training for a week or two in warm weather conditions, giving you ample time for your private life as well as training.

There, a weekly mileage of 600-700 miles in two weeks would be a fantastic foundation for the coming season. Run 3 x 1 hr, swim twice a week if possible.

You can find detailed information about running, swimming and cycling training in Chapter 8. It is also important not to forget stretching and strengthening the most stressed parts of the body. The months of March and April have the highest training volume.

Day	Training	Comments
Mon.	–	Stretching, sauna
Tues.	70 min. run	Warm-up with technique drills, intervals 1,2,3,4,5,4,3,2,1 min., tempo runs, T5-T6, 1min. rests **Core training**
Wed.	60 min. swim	Technique exercises, intervals, 4 x 100 yds, 4 x 200 yds, T5-T6, **core training**
Thur.	75 min. run	Relaxed, T3
Fri.	30-40 miles cycling	Gentle bike ride, T2
Sat.	40-50 miles cycling 60 min. swimming	Relaxed ride, T3 S. Endurance, warm-up/down, 4 x 500 yds, T3-T4 **core training**
Sun.	60 min. running + 30 miles cycling **Total: about 12 hrs**	Relaxed running, T3, and equally relaxed cycling, T3

Fig. 12: Suggested training for training week 2, without training camp, i.e. ***"normal" week****.*

For weeks 1 and 3, January's guidelines.

Adapt your training to your individual capabilities!
These training suggestions are literally only intended to be just that.

Day	Training	Comments
Mon.	–	Strengthening exercises
Tues.	40 min. run	Relaxed, T3, no speedwork
Wed.	45 min. swim	Technique exercises, intervals, T4
Thur.	–	
Fri.	25 miles cycling	Gentle bike ride, T2
Sat.	40 min. cycling	Relaxed bike ride, T3
	50 min. swimming	S. Endurance, warm up/down, 4 x 500 yds T3
Sun.	50 min. running	Jogging T2
	Total: about 6 hours	

Figure 13: The fourth week (regeneration week).

April:
Now, or preferably two weeks earlier, the second part of the preparation period starts. The foundations for our three disciplines are laid. Now that you have a good basis, training gets one level quicker, but the volume does not increase. We should be thinking of training more frequently at a quick to fast pace.

It now becomes important to practice the transitions, particularly the transition from cycling to running. In the case of cycling, time trials and shorter tempo rides are now brought in. In the case of running, tempo runs are now included, although only in the first three training weeks. In the fourth week, the regeneration week, all tempo work should be dropped.

In the case of swimming, the key sessions consist either of longer intervals, 4 x 500 yards at competition pace, or they can even be 2 x 1,000 yards.

Day	Training	Comments
Mon.	–	Stretching, sauna
Tues.	75 min. run	Warm-up/warm down, 3 x 2,000 yards tempo runs, T6+, Stretching, **core training**
Wed.	2-3 hour cycling	Relaxed, T3 bike ride, **core training**
Thur.	60 min. swimming	Technique drills, intervals, 5 x 300 yards, T4-T5
Fri.	–	
Sat.	65 miles cycling	R with 3 x 20 min. tempo rides, T6-T7

	60 min. swimming	Endurance, warm-up/down, 4 x 500 yds, T3 **core training**
Sun.	12 mile run	Relaxed, T3
	Total: 11 hr training	

Fig. 13: Suggested Training for week 2, without training camp, i.e., "normal+ week."

For weeks 1,3, and 4, see January's guidelines.

May:

In May, we gradually get used to the race pace. In cycling, we progressively approach the desired competition pace by carrying out 3 x 30 min, 2 x 40 min, 2 x 50 min and finally 3 x 50 min at race pace. Shorter distances in the time trials should, of course, also be appreciably faster.

In running, competition pace is not that much faster than training pace. Nevertheless, try to raise your anaerobic threshold with interval and tempo endurance runs. Suitable examples are 6-8 x 1,000 yards in 10 km pace, 2-3 x 5 km at 90% of race pace with jogging intervals of 1-2 miles.

As in April, swimming consists of intervals and endurance swimming.
   The bike-run transition should be practiced at least once a week, aiming for a quick transition.

You can try a short triathlon competition as a dress rehearsal.

Day	Training	Comments
Mon.	–	Stretching, sauna
Tues.	60 min. run + 1 hour Swim	Fartlek, S. intervals
Wed.	2 hours cycling	Fast ride, T5, core training
Thur.	–	
Fri.	2 hours cycling	Relaxed bike ride, T3
Sat.	1 hour swimming	With short, quick intervals
Sun.	Test competition	Olympic distance, 90-95%, core training
	Total: 9 hrs training	

Highest Volumes and Intensities

Day	Training	Comments
Mon.	–	Stretching, sauna
Tues.	1 hour Swim	3 x 800 yards, Ironman competition pace, if possible in open water
Wed.	1hr 50 running	Speed endurance runs, 3 x 3,000 yards, T3, **core training**
Thur.	–	
Fri.	2 hours cycling 1.5 hours running	cycling, T3 + running, T3, core training
Sat.	1.5 hours swimming	Interval training, T3
Sun.	4 hours cycling **Total: 12 hrs training**	Warm up/down, 3 x 50 mins race pace + stretching, core training

Pre-Competition Week: Slow reduction of volume and intensity

Day	Training	Comments
Mon.	–	Stretching, sauna
Tues.	1 hour Swim	1.2 mile endurance swim at race pace, in open water
Wed.	2 hours running	With short fartlek, core training
Thur.	–	
Fri.	2 hours cycling + 1.5 hours running	1 hour cycling, T6, competition pace + running, T2, **core training**
Sat.	1 hour swimming	Relaxed, T3, long intervals 5 x 400 yards
Sun.	1 hour cycling + 1 hour running **Total: 9.5 hrs training**	Both T3, **core training**

Ironman 70.3 Competition Week

Day	Training	Comments
Mon.	–	Stretching, sauna
Tues.	45 min. run + 12.4 miles cycling	With 3,000 yard tempo run, T6, + 6.2 mile tempo bike ride, T6, to empty glycogen reserves, **core training**
Wed.	45 min swimming	With short intervals, e.g. 4 x 50 yard tempo, otherwise relaxed
Thur.	45 min cycling	T1
Fri.	–	
Sat.	1.2/56/13.1 miles	**Ironman 70.3 Competition**
Sun.		Swimming, T1 or 15 miles cycling, T1

Figure 15: Possible training schedules for the last four weeks before the Ironman 70.3 during the competition period.

Competition Period: June to September

June:
The first Ironman 70.3 should be followed by two weeks of regenerative training. You should also take it easy for a whole week, followed by a second week where you return to regenerative training T1-T2. After this, you can train normally again, i.e., R, R, N. (R stands for regeneration week and N for normal week.)

You may also compete in more short and medium triathlons in the months of **August and September**.

As shown in the previous chapter, the training of an ambitious triathlete can be organized in order for them to finish in around 5-6 hours. The example below shows us another way to approach the training for an Ironman 70.3.

7.1.5   A practical training example

Patricia's (W40) training, as well as being geared toward the Ironman 70.3 (in 5:24hr) was also geared to the Ironman (12:10hr) that took place four weeks later. She first took up the triathlon four years ago. She usually trained with her partner Pierre.

Annual training volume: 140 miles swimming, 2,500 miles cycling and 1,000 miles running.

She does triathlons "because I wanted to keep fit and then ambition took over. Triathlon is also a great sport as it is so varied."

Preparation Period: 8 months

Competition period: 3 months

Transition period: 1 month

Patricia's training in the last five weeks before the Ironman 70.3 in Switzerland looked like this:

1st week of May: (9 hours training)
Focus: 1st week of May short triathlon

Date: from		to				Week:					
Day	Weight lb	S Dist. yards	Time	C Dist. miles	Time	R Dist. mile	time	Other sporting activity	Comments	Resting pulse rate	Weight lb
Mon.		3,000							technique		
Tues.						8		+ strength			
Wed.		3,000							lots of arm work		
Thurs.				50					slipstream		
Fri.		2,500							Technique/paddles		
Sat.						15			Mountain running		
Sun.											
Totals:		8,500		50		23					

2nd week of May: (10 hours training)
Focus: 2nd week of May

Date: from		to				Week:					
Day	Weight lb	S Dist. yards	Time	C Dist. miles	Time	R Dist. mile	time	Other sporting activity	Comments	Resting pulse rate	Weight lb
Mon.				50					Intervals		
Tues.						6.2			Fartlek		
Wed.											
Thurs.				40	relaxed						
Fri.		2,200							Relaxed, sprints		
Sat.									Test competition		
Sun.				25		10			Relaxed		
Totals:		2,200		115		16.2					

3rd week of May: (14 hours training)
Focus: cycling

Date: from		to				Week:					
Day	Weight lb	S Dist. yards	Time	C Dist. miles	Time	R Dist. mile	time	Other sporting activity	Comments	Resting pulse rate	Weight lb
Mon.		3,000		34		6.2			S 5 x 400		
Tues.											
Wed.		2,400				7.5			S endurance		
Thurs.		600						Pilates			
Fri.											
Sat.				93		1.5			Bike-run "brick"		
Sun.											
Totals:		6,000		127		15.2					

4th week of May: (16 hours training)

Date: from	to						Week:			
Day	Weight lb	S Dist. yards	Time	C Dist. miles	Time	R Dist. mile	time	Other sporting activity	Comments	Resting pulse rate	Wght lb
Mon.											
Tues.				30		9			Running B. endurance		
Wed.		3,400							Tempo training		
Thurs.				55		5			Cycling + running		
Fri.		2,500				6.2			Different paces		
Sat.									Slipstream		
Sun.				60		14.3	gentle				
Totals:		5,900		145		34.5					

1st Week of June Competition Week:
Focus: IRONMAN 70.3 Switzerland

Date: from	to						Week:			
Day	Weight lb	S Dist. yards	Time	C Dist. miles	Time	R Dist. mile	time	Other sporting activity	Comments	Resting pulse rate	Wght lb
Mon.		1,200									
Tues.				23		4			C quick R fartlek		
Wed.		1,650	Neo								
Thurs.				12		2		C + R	C relaxed R quick		
Fri.											
Sat.				12					Spinning™		
Sun.		1,800*	29	60	3hr04	13.1	1:43	5:24	Rapperswil 1,100 HM		
Totals:		4,650		107		19					

* swimming course shortened due to very cold water (57°F)

7.1.6 Patricia: "I still have so much strength left"

Patricia was supervised as much as possible by her partner Pierre, who was preparing for the Ironman Zurich.

Pierre: This is our home competition. We see many familiar faces, like a big family. Some we know, some we had seen before. I would actually like to start, but it doesn't fit in with my training schedule. I feel jittery and the atmosphere gets to me.

Patricia: Still five minutes to go. This is it. My thoughts revolve around the water. One part of me is amazed that I have to go in. Because of the temperature, the swimming course was even shortened. I am so nervous about getting into the water. On the swimming coach's advice, I am wearing three swimming caps. Two are better than one, and three are better than two. Somehow I manage to forget this unpleasant pre-race anxiety. Have I trained enough? Will I fight like a tiger? Have I eaten enough? Two minutes. There someone is still talking to me! I'm so happy; it's so great. We are going to enjoy the race. I give him one of my swimming caps and he is gone.

One minute, I'm going in, my breathing is slowing down, relaxed in breaststroke forward, not too far forward, pure mental training, I'm not alone, I want to be alone, far away – Starting signal – AT LAST!

Starting signal! The arms fly and splash, the triathletes struggle through the cold water. After a while, the field starts to spread out. Who would want to get into water at 60° F?

How beautiful, nobody is jostling. I think that everyone is too busy ignoring the cold. Don't start too quickly, but slowly, deliberately start to pull with the arms, and swim strongly towards the end. I think of the technique drills I have done, high elbows, body rotation, etc. Soon I can no longer feel my feet and my fingers are cramping. It was a wise decision to shorten the course.

A clever triathlete once gave me some equally clever advice along the way. You can give your all on the cycling course. He had not mentioned that there could be a problem getting to the bike. My feet are frozen! I finally make it to my bike, but don't take off my wetsuit (this will annoy me later!), and when running out of the transition zone, I have to get the bananas that have fallen out of my jersey. But I will give it my all – this is my motto – once I can feel my feet again!

People's faces show how cold it is! However, there are some who are running incredibly relaxed to the transition zone, encouraged by us spectators.

Cycling! I put my feet to the pedals, paying attention to my pedaling and heart rates. My body gives its all. Why am I always overtaken?! Damn, the others are fast. You know yourself. Take your time. You still have to run; that is your strong point. Finally we are going up! I try to climb relaxed up the hill and enjoy the shouts of encouragement like: "You're looking good," "Bravo!" I let the words drive me on. How awesome.

Watching cycling is so frustrating. They go by so quickly. But I do have time to have a coffee, chat with friends who are also not competing and calculate when the leaders will show up again in the transition zone. Just as when one is competing oneself, one is always calculating.

How quickly the 56 miles pass. Although, others were even quicker! During the last 6 miles, I am looking forward to the running! I am pleased that this is only a test run. I must not put pressure on myself. During running I am near the crowd, I hear: "Come on Patricia," I see familiar faces! But where are the faces that I REALLY know?

The clever triathlete, mentioned above, told me that I should run the first 15 minutes fast and then slow down. No sooner said than done. My legs feel great! I can run off immediately. After 13 minutes I look for someone else's legs, which become my pacemakers. I now spend my time behind the chosen ones. I am delighted that I feel so good, smile at the spectators and must always check that I don't kick the other's legs.

I'm not a very good spectator and have just missed the equally poor future female spectator in the transition zone. I wait with triathlon friends on the running course and puzzle over what has happened to our protégée.

I'm off! I stick to my heart rate. I feel as though I am on a treadmill. If I continue to run with this heart rate, I will be faster than my last time in Locarno. Perhaps I will see what I can do after the third lap.

M. Nüsken

Ouch! I fell! Up the step, there were cobblestones underneath and I stumbled over. While I was falling, I luckily decided on a dive roll. Now my hips hurt a little but I didn't fall flat on my face. I just have to run a few pulse beats faster.

There they are, our friends! One is still kissing half her family, the other is posing for a photo. There she comes, it looks as though she is following advice.

Last lap. In front there are a few W40s. I'm going to catch them, yes I am. Forget the advice. I feel brilliant (where is the next Ironman 70.3? I want more). Pull the knees up, keep your ankles relaxed, your back straight. By controlling my body posture, I always run faster. I'm really going for it now! Why didn't I swim and cycle faster? I still have so much strength.

They fly into the hall. Have I made a miscalculation? Am I waiting one circuit too soon? It's true, being a spectator needs practice too!

Run into the ice rink. God it's beautiful! A fantastic run into the finish. Music, people, and most of all, it's cool! I've done it!

Henry is another example of an ambitious triathlete. His best time is in the region of 5:16-5:24. For the Ironman 70.3 in Rapperswil, Switzerland, his time was 5:16 hrs, and five weeks later at the Ironman in Klagenfurt, Austria, it was 11:19 hrs. Only one week before Rapperswil, he also ran the medium distance (1.2/56/13.1 miles) in Linz, Austria, in 5:16 hours. Later in the season, in September, even after cutting back on training, Henry finished a 1.5/56/13 mile race in 5:24 hrs.

Henry's Annual Training Volume:

Swimming: 80 miles
Cycling: 3-4,000 miles
Running: 1,500 miles
Age Group: M60, 25 years as an active triathlete
Speciality: Training only in the basic endurance zone, in his comfort zone.

7.2   Training for Performance-Oriented Athletes (P: 4:50-4:10 hours)

For performance-oriented triathletes, a whole series of very positive circumstances must come together for performances between 4:10 hrs and 4:50 hrs to be achieved.

As well as the time required and great endurance, the athlete must also be able to cope physically with the training volumes in order to prepare himself or herself for the more intense racing. This usually requires one developmental year in triathlon.

This group is where the real winners can be found, and where training must be much harder in order to achieve the desired times in competition. No triathlete will achieve these demanding times on basic endurance training alone, as performed by triathlon novices. Several years' experience and significant talent are also required.

In general, the statements for the ambitious triathletes category still apply, just at a higher level. That does not necessarily involve greatly increasing training volumes in each discipline, just that the basic swimming, cycling and running speeds are higher than those of ambitious athletes. This can be seen clearly in the very interesting training schedule of Oliver Reitenbach, below. He gets by with only 90-112 miles of swimming training annually, and with this achieves performances that others cannot even manage on twice as much training. This is quite clearly because of his superior natural talents.

7.2.1 Required race split times

4:10-4:50 hr	
Swimming 1.2 miles	25-33 min
Cycling 56 miles	2:21-2:35 hours
Running 13.1 miles	1:18-1:35 hours
Transition times	Approx. 6 mins

Fig. 16: Target times for the medium distance.

7.2.2 Training example – Oliver

We would like to offer a specific training example of a triathlete in this category who is capable of achieving times of **4:10-4:20 hrs** in an Ironman 70.3. His Ironman time of less than 9 hours shows just how good he could be. His time of 8:47 hours does not quite put him up there with the pros, but he could hold his own with many semi-pros.

Oliver is also a 38-year-old man who actively practiced sport throughout his childhood. Since the age of six, he participated in competitive swimming. He has been an active triathlete since age 23. He is a complete triathlete, who has many strengths but no weaknesses. He is exceptionally strong in all three disciplines and manages this on relatively low training volumes, especially in swimming.

Oliver, born in 1967, is a thoroughly nice guy, who does triathlons answers: "First of all as a sporting challenge, then out of enjoyment of the sport, with the possibility of pushing my performance limits."

His training in the whole year are in the region of:
      100-120 miles swimming
      3,800 miles cycling
      1,250 miles running

K. Reitenbach

This equates to 430 annual training hours, or 8.3 hours per week. In comparison, 40-year-old Patricia from Switzerland trains 375 hours annually (7.2 hours per week) and the now 60-year-old Henry trains around 410 hours annually (8 hours per week). Although there is not a great deal of difference between the training load of the three triathletes, Oliver is in a class of his own. He has been blessed with more endurance talent than Patricia and Henry. This is also true from the point of view that Patricia, as a woman, gets a 10% advantage, as does Henry on account of his age.

However, the main point is that each athlete is very happy with his or her performance.

These are Oliver's best times in triathlon competitions:

10km run	35:30 min
Half marathon	1:18 hours
25 miles cycling	1 hour
3,000m swimming	13:20 min (without Neoprene wetsuit)

His annual training structure:

Preparation phase:	5 months
Competition phase:	4-5 months
Transition phase:	2-3 months

In winter/spring, running emphasis is focused on the basics. Cycling is emphasized in the spring, mainly over the Easter vacation. Swimming is only trained shortly before important competitions, in the manner outlined below. Otherwise, Oliver only does a one-hour swim workout each week. During competition season, he does around 11-12 workouts per week if the combined training is calculated as separate sessions.

Oliver's training plan for the last four weeks before the medium distance

Emphasis: Cycling   Training 16 h

Date: from		to			Week:						
Day	Weight lb	S Dist. yards	Time	C Dist. miles	Time	R Dist. mile	time	Other sporting activity	Comments	Resting pulse rate	Weight lb
Mon.	161	3,300	0:48	84	3:30			Canal swimming		38/128	
Tues.						13.1	1:33	Fartlek		38/142	
Wed.				50	2:28					37/123	
Thurs.								Rest day			
Fri.		2,200	0:28	39	1:50					38/123	
Sat.				100	3:53	3.1	0:22	Brick training		38/130	
Sun.	161	4,400	1:00			9.3	1:07			38/130	
Totals:		9,900		283		25.5					

Emphasis: Cycling-Running   Training 15 h

Date: from		to			Week:						
Day	Weight lb	S Dist. yards	Time	C Dist. miles	Time	R Dist. mile	time	Other sporting activity	Comments	Resting pulse rate	Weight lb
Mon.								Rest day			
Tues.	163	4,400	1:00	28	1:24	9	1:02			37/120	163
Wed.								Rest day			
Thurs.		2,200	0:30	59	2:55	7.5	0:50		quickly up mountains	37/132	
Fri.	161			60	3:00				Quick and even	37/130	163
Sat.				22	1:15	1.5	0:09.30		Race preparation Brick training	37/135	
Sun.		1,400	0:17	26	1:03	6.5	37:50		Triathlon competition		
Totals:		8,000		195		24.5					

Emphasis: Brick training   Training 13 h

Date: from		to			Week:					
Day	Weight lb	S Dist. yards	Time	C Dist. miles	Time	R Dist. mile	time	Other sporting activity	Comments	Resting pulse rate	Weight lb
Mon.	161	1,650	0:22	22	1:15	2.8	0:20	Regeneration		39/120	161
Tues.								Rest day			
Wed.						9.3	1:03		Relaxed	38/133	
Thurs.		4,300	0:45	19	0:55				Brick training	38/130	
Fri.								Rest day			
Sat.		0.93	0:22	19	1:00	3.1	0:20		Brick training	38/125	
Sun.	161	1,000	5:10	112	510	13.1	1:35		Intensive brick training	38/145	163
Totals:		6,950		172		28.3					

Emphasis: Ironman 70.3 or Medium Distance Triathlon

Date: from		to			Week:					
Day	Weight lb	S Dist. yards	Time	C Dist. miles	Time	R Dist. mile	time	Other sporting activity	Comments	Resting pulse rate	Weight lb
Mon.	163							Rest day		39	163
Tues.				21	1:17				Relaxed	38/110	
Wed.								Rest day		38	
Thurs.		3,300	0:52	7.5		7.5	0:49		Canal swimming	38/125	
Fri.				15	0:49	1.50	0:10		Intensive brick training	38/138	
Sat.				25	1:30	3.1	0:20.30			38/130	
Sun.		2,100	26	56	2:21	13.1	1:18		Medium distance 4:10h		
Totals:		5,400		117		25.2			Approx. 11h		

7.3 Doris: "Florida: bring it on!"

Doris is a performance-oriented triathlete, 36 years old and has been an enthusiastic triathlete since 2005. She caught the triathlon "bug" in 2004, when she was a spectator at the Ironman Austria. Doris' sporting background is very interesting: She comes from a very different sport – ice hockey. She played in the women's national ice hockey league and won several championship titles with her team.

She took up triathlon quite late. In response to the question of what she finds so fascinating about triathlon, Doris says: "It is not so easy to change from a speed strength sport to an endurance sport. On an ice hockey team, you are always only as good as the whole team; you win and lose together as a team. As a non-swimmer, I was also looking for a new challenge. I could not imagine running for a whole hour either, but where there's a will, there's a way."

Doris' first triathlon was actually the Ironman Austria, which she successfully completed in 12:01:45. Only one year later, she was able to reduce her time to 11:24:31h and in 2007, her brilliant time of 10:25:27h appeared in the results list. This time enabled Doris to qualify for the world championships in Hawaii. In the Ironman 70.3 in St. Pölten (Austria), Doris qualified for the world championships in Clearwater Beach with second place in her age group in 5:14:09h (in adverse weather conditions). At the world championships, she achieved a fantastic 4:51:32h.

Her athletic strengths are her endurance and perseverance, consistency, mental strength and her realistic and specific goal-setting. Doris believes that her weakness is that she is sometimes too impatient. Aren't we all? However, especially in endurance sports, patience is required, for in order to "build high towers, we must spend a long time laying the foundations."

Doris used the Ironman 70.3 as a preparation race for the Ironman Austria.

The average training load, including stretching and stabilization exercises, lies in the region of 16.5 hours per week. Only in competition weeks is the amount reduced to six hours.

Here is her report of her experience in the Ironman 70.3 in St. Pölten:

"I finished with three seconds to spare!"

From a training point of view, the last week before the Ironman 70.3 was a very nice, calm week. My coach cut back my race-week training, so that I had enough time for my recovery. Nevertheless, I was very tense because this was my first race of the season, and I had absolutely no references to go on except my tests on the treadmill.

The night before, I didn't sleep very well and on the race day itself, I was extremely nervous although I knew that my training and preparation was optimal. I naturally also had an important goal: qualification for the world championships in Clearwater Beach, Florida, in November 2007, for which my training had been directed.

Suddenly, a few minutes before the start, a thunderstorm broke out. Stormy winds whipped torrential rain at us until it was almost horizontal. We athletes escaped into the water and waited there for the start and spectators and supporters tried to find cover behind bushes and trees. The water in the lake was so whipped up by the wind that the swimmers could no longer see the first buoys. The water-start went smoothly, but unfortunately I could not find my usual good rhythm. The "frog pond" in St. Pölten, also known as the bathing lake, was very grim. After about 1,000 yards, I reached the first exit, which was followed by a run of about 300 yards over a bridge and a tarmac path to the second lake, in which we had to swim another 1,000 yards.

Roelie

When I left the water, I was leading in my age group and in the transition zone, which was now completely under water, I tried to free my feet from grime and mud to jump quickly onto my bike.

In the meantime, the rain had stopped again, but there was water everywhere and the route was extremely slippery. Already at the first roundabout, I had to brake suddenly as unfortunately one of the many falls of the day had occurred. On the highway, we then went towards Krems. It was a great experience. I could apply the right amount of pressure, and it was naturally a cool feeling to sit on a bike and have the whole highway to ourselves. The wave start – divided according to age groups – was beneficial in that it ensured an absolutely fair race as far as slipstream was concerned. It was each man or woman for himself or herself.

The bike course was very selective, and due to the wet and dirty course, it was very dangerous to ride. I had to ride the downhill sections especially carefully so I did not – like so many athletes – land in the field. The black sky above me made me fear the worst, and my fears were confirmed. A thunderstorm dashed my hopes of a great bike time. What happened next is hard to even describe.

Within seconds, the road turned into a small stream. The rain fell so hard I could barely make out the road. It was all I could do to keep my bike and myself on the road. It was like a bad movie. I just thought, "What on earth are you doing here?" But the thought was forgotten just as quickly, as I knew that it was the same for my competitors and I was therefore also able to maintain my lead after 56 miles on the bike. It would naturally just be impossible now to achieve the time I had expected. But the priority was to reach the transition zone healthy and uninjured.

I was really happy to have made it without falling, and I now only had to run 13.1 miles. I felt very good and knew I would definitely have a great running split. This turned out to be the case, 1:39:19 h for the half marathon and with a negative running split, too, which I was very satisfied with. At the start of the half marathon, I knew that I was still in the lead, and I also knew that a ticket to the World Championships in Clearwater Beach was within my reach! Just after the first turn in the Government District, the future age group winner overtook me and the future third-place athlete was suddenly breathing down my neck. I knew that to qualify for the world championships I had to finish second. She was not going to take it away from me. I finished with three seconds to spare!

8 Improving Your Performance

8.1 Become an Ironman 70.3

In training, there is no sure-fire formula for triathlon success. A training plan that works for one athlete cannot just be transferred as-is to another athlete. Even for professional athletes, this does not work. What benefits one may be too much, or even too little, for another. For this reason, we repeat the advice:

Every triathlete must discover the capabilities of his/her individual environment!

We therefore need to listen to our bodies, our physical condition and our performance level, and in the process, abide by the important principles outlined in this book. Our training recommendations to achieve our great Ironman 70.3 objective are just that – recommendations. They are not set in stone and it is up to the athlete to be self-critical and to enjoy the sport without letting it harm those around him/her. This will lead to personal success, but not necessarily to victory.

The basic speed is primarily a matter of talent, which we are either born with or not. Endurance is different. It doesn't matter how old, tall, heavy or fit we are; endurance can be improved by training.

By improving endurance, we can push our limits!

For many triathletes this is one of many reasons they compete in triathlon races. Anyone who tells friends, acquaintances, colleagues or relatives they are a triathlete will almost certainly be asked: "So, have you done an Ironman yet?"

Yes, most people associate the words "Ironman" and "Hawaii" with triathlon. Ironmen and Ironwomen are endurance royalty. These distances, including the Ironman 70.3, can be accomplished not only by semi and full professionals, but by anyone who has two healthy legs – as Henry puts it so well – and we already learned from the experiences by the beginners in chapter 6. Given the amount of time people spend sitting in front of the TV these days, it is no longer a question of finding the time needed to train for these distances, but only a question of will and motivation.

There is only one basic prerequisite: good health. We should have be checked regularly by a medical professional. Even if you have no health problems, you should visit your physician once a year in order to get a general check-up and blood test.

Let's now address some essential training elements more thoroughly:

What happens to our bodies during endurance training?

The body initially reacts to a hard training stimulus with a state of fatigue, a loss of energy. If this is followed by two days or so of rest, **supercompensation** sets in. This is a physical state in which the energy level is higher than it was at the start due to the body's adaptation process. In this way, the body prepares itself to deal with new loads. However, if the body is not given enough time for regeneration, there is a risk of overtraining and immediate injury. Adequate regeneration is therefore essential for the training effect to occur, meaning that without regeneration, performance improvement is impossible.

The recovery phase is equally important. Well-trained triathletes do not necessarily need two days of absolute rest in order to train. A heavy workout should therefore be followed by short, regenerative workouts. Long, slow training has little effect (they are more useful for muscular adaptation), they should not be considered regenerative purely because of their length.

So which principles should our training follow?

The secret is to alternate endurance and speed training.

For Ironman 70.3, primarily train the cardiovascular system and metabolism, as they are the most important factors in long-distance running. In addition to this, there is also a specific swimming, cycling and running pace that must be achieved in competition. A lot of endurance training without tempo training will allow us to finish the race, but not to improve our performance.

Therefore, after **the basics**, we also **train competition pace**.
    However, we must assume that our prospects of success grow with a good basic endurance foundation.

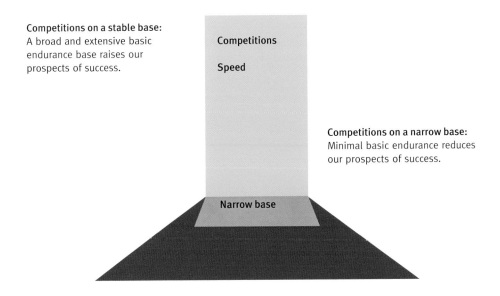

Competitions on a stable base:
A broad and extensive basic endurance base raises our prospects of success.

Competitions

Speed

Competitions on a narrow base:
Minimal basic endurance reduces our prospects of success.

Narrow base

So, once the foundation – the basic endurance – has been laid, we should proceed as follows:

For each discipline, perform a long endurance workout in the basic endurance zones T2-T3 and an intensive workout in the higher zones T5-T7. As far as workouts in T1-T3 are concerned, it should be possible to chat comfortably with others. In zones T5-T7, conversation is either only monosyllabic or impossible.

If we can only say a few syllables while breathing heavily, we are at the anaerobic threshold, approximately T6. Very performance-oriented athletes or sprint triathlon specialists only train above this threshold over short intervals.

Ambitious and performance-oriented triathletes should heed the following advice:
- **At least one regenerative training day before and after an intensive workout.**
- **If you neglect recovery, you risk overtraining.**

Discipline	T1 Regenerative Workouts	T1-T5 Workouts Full Conversation possible	T5-T7 Workouts Only monosyllabic conversation possible
Swimming	Technique training	Technique training Endurance method Sprints, Neoprene swimming	Intervals 100-300 yds Tests over 1,000 yards or 30 min.
Biking	At most 90 min. gentle bike rides	Long cycling workouts	60, 90 min. hill intervals, 2-3 x 10-15 min., intervals 4-5 x 3-6 miles
Running	At most 45 min. gentle endurance runs	Long running workouts	6-8 x 1,000 yards, 5 min. jog, 3 x 2 miles, 5 min jog, tempo endurance runs 3-6 miles, long fartlek 1-3-5-7-5-3-1 min.

Fig. 17: Distribution of T1-T8 workouts.

8.2 Avoid typical training errors

Soon we will explore in more detail how your athletic potential can be fulfilled. Below we briefly list ways it can be limited. More information can be found on this in Hermann Aschwer's book *The Complete Guide to Triathlon Training*.

The following points will greatly limit your success:

- no training plan
- too much training
- training too hard
- too many competitions
- inadequate regeneration
- bad diet
- incorrect attitude toward sport
- lack of motivation and/or sense of purpose
- insufficient stretching and/or strengthening exercises

sportfotograph

By following these examples, sooner or later you will suffer from injury, overtraining and loss of motivation.

The important thing here is that every triathlete finds what suits him. While one triathlete can compete in 15 competitions and another 10 running races without burning out, others can only cope with 4-5 triathlons per season. This is the case with Marlies and Henry. Marlies can manage 20 or more competitions, while Henry's limit is 8-10 triathlons and 4-5 running races.

All we can do is give you tips for your everyday training. It is up to the athlete to be responsible, constructively critical, and take into account his strengths and weaknesses, his positive and negative external conditions and make the best of his possibilities.

Another tip for masters (age 40 and above): The high training loads (T7-T8) are less suitable for this age group. Masters triathletes also need more time for regeneration. You can read more about this in Henry's book *Lifelong Training Triathlon - Advanced Training for Masters*.

8.3 Improve your swimming

In Ironman 70.3 the swimming always takes place in open water. It is extremely rare to find medium distance events where the swimming takes place in an open-air swimming pool. That means that in colder weather a Neoprene wetsuit should be worn, as it considerably improves swimming position in the water, which is positively reflected in swimming times. Experience shows that average swimmers benefit more than good swimmers. Time advantages of 2-3 minutes per mile are realistic. For average swimmers, there is the added advantage that the Neoprene wetsuit helps to improve body tension.

Below are short, basic tips for swimming in the Neoprene wetsuit, as the book *The Complete Guide to Triathlon Training* has already very thoroughly dealt with the swimming program and swimming in open water.

8.3.1 Open water swimming

When swimming in open water, pay particular attention to the following: Well before a competition (at least 2-3 weeks), every season you should refamiliarize yourself with the wetsuit and also with swimming in open water. This also applies to very good swimmers who have, until now, been training in the swimming pool.

You need to get used to the turbidity of open water. It is not uncommon for great swimmers to be unable to transfer their swimming performances to the lake. It can even happen that in the first yards of swimming, they are completely unable to cope with the turbid water as they find it very unpleasant some even give up completely and pull out of the competition after a few yards.

- The tight fit of the Neoprene can lead to anxiety and restricted breathing. This feeling will disappear with time.

- Possible pre-season weight changes can mean that the wetsuit is too big or too small, and a certain amount of familiarization is required.

- You should apply Vaseline around your neck area before putting on the wetsuit in order to avoid unpleasant chafing.

Training

- You should also train several times without the wetsuit, otherwise technique will be neglected.

- It should be worn for regeneration workouts, e.g., one day after intensive bike or running workouts.

- Carry out interval training again and again, also in open water. Either use a fixed geographical feature (lake inlet, certain sections, from landing stage to landing stage) or a timer, a watch or even just count your breathing, as Henry often does. Start at a 50 or 100 breath pace, then the same amount again, relaxed.

- The start and the associated jostling can be practiced in the swimming pool. 10-12 triathletes stand in front of one swimming lane, and after a simulated starting signal, they then start to swim intervals of 5 x 200 yards.

- Another training aspect that is often neglected is that the start in open water swimming often takes place on a pebbly or stony beach. Good preparation for this is to walk barefoot on pebbly surfaces.

- A pontoon start can be practiced very well from the starting blocks of the pool.

A little more about the swimming technique itself

- The ability to breathe on both sides gives you a big advantage when it comes to finding your bearings in open water swimming.

- Even very experienced triathletes may still have problems with "catching" water. This phase takes place after the immersion and extension phases of the arm. It involves bending the elbow but never pulling it back. This means specifically that the elbow is vertical from the moment of flexion until the completion of the pulling phase. At the same time, the forearm is exactly diagonal to the direction of movement. Now the thrust phase starts. The water resistance must be felt as strongly as possible throughout the underwater phase. We pull ourselves forward with the palm of the hand and with the cross-sectional area of the forearm and upper arm. In a three-phase pull in the clear water of a swimming pool, this process can be seen very clearly. The better you are at catching water, the fewer arm strokes you will need to cover a given distance (e.g., 50 yards) and the faster your swimming speed will be.

- Counting how many breaths you take per length will tell you how effective your water catching is. Good swimmers are characterized by their efficient water catching ability. Average swimmers must work hard on this at the start of the season. It is often possible to do this just with technique training, training monitoring and frequent swim training.

- Another technical swimming error is high head carriage. This causes the lower body to sink, which increases water resistance and makes you swim slower. So, immerse your head until the surface of the water lies between your middle of your head and your forehead. In open water, a high head carriage is only necessary for about five breaths, or 15 strokes.

- The third main crawl technique error is the lateral deviation of the hips due to inadequate body tension. This must be worked on by means of strengthening exercises. The Neoprene wetsuit helps you avoid this error as it increases body tension.

Finally, another general swimming problem:
Triathlete Jan writes: "…cycling and running are no problem. The only problem is that I swim too slowly. It takes me one hour to swim 1.5 miles, without stopping. How can I improve?"

www.sailfish.com

The short answer is: If you always train at the same tempo, you will be able to scrape by and finish, but your performances will not improve. In order to swim faster you need to cover shorter intervals of 8 x 100 yds, 10 x 50 yds + 4 x 200 yds or similar intervals, in which you will swim more quickly than endurance swimming. Then rest for 15 and 30 seconds respectively.

The rule is: The shorter the interval length, the higher the speed. Endurance swimming in the form of 4 x 400 yds or 2 x 800 yds should also be performed once a week.

8.3.2   The 12 core swim workouts

These 12 workouts can be trained in the last 12 weeks before the Ironman 70.3. Race pace is what you want to achieve in the actual Ironman 70.3. Every workout naturally also includes an adequate warm-up and cool-down. Normal training, consisting of interval and endurance training, should be performed alongside this core training.

Week	Distances	Explanations
1	2,000 yards	Endurance
2	2 x 1,100 yards	Even pace
3	3 x 900 yards	Increase second half to race pace over 1.2 miles
4	4 x 700 yards	As week 3
5		Regeneration, only relaxed swimming
6	8 x 300 yards	Alternate relaxed and tempo
7	2 x 1,000 yards	Increase second half
8	6 x 400 yards	3 x tempo, 1 x relaxed, 2 x tempo
9		Regeneration, only relaxed swimming
10	4 x 700 yards	Race pace, maybe even faster
11	3 x 900 yards	Race pace, maybe even faster
12	2,000 yards	Race pace, maybe even faster
IM 70.3 week	Optional	

Fig.18: The 12 core swim workouts.

If you want to improve your swimming, technique training is your first priority. If you swim lengths with an incorrect technique, you are wasting your time, as endurance can also be trained very well by cycling and running.

Basic principle

Make the water your friend and don't see it as your enemy.

The most important thing in swimming is getting a feel for the water. For this, the hands must be clean (don't put lotion on beforehand), so they can sense the water properly. Marlies always washes her hands before swim training, and between lengths, she often stops briefly at the side of the pool and rubs the palms of her hands on the rough tiles to make them as sensitive as possible.

Exercises to improve your feel for the water

- Play with the water, try to hold it and catch it in order to pull yourself forward.

- Swim holding tennis balls: After warming up, swim for 100 yards with tennis balls in your hands, then swim again for 100 yards without them.

If you swim with tennis balls, you have the feeling you are not moving. When you swim without them afterward your hands feel enormous and you will notice that you can "pull" the water more effectively.

- Count the strokes per length: Your aim is to reduce the number of strokes. If you need about 20 strokes, then concentrate on pulling through efficiently and powerfully in order to reduce the number to 18 (or less).

As far as breathing is concerned, breathe out completely under water. Many beginners make the mistake of holding their breath, but once you start to breathe in, you will not be able to breathe out completely. You cannot breathe in and out at the same time. Instead, imagine that you are blowing the water away from you as you breathe out.

You have to really concentrate when you are swimming if you want to improve, but when cycling and running, you can let your mind wander. When swimming, it is only by kicking your legs and pulling with a few square inches of hand, forearm and upper arm surface that you can propel yourself forward.

8.4 Improve your cycling

In Ironman 70.3, you spend 50-55% of the race on your bike. You need a solid foundation to be able to ride for 56 miles and do well in the overall race. You should get a few thousand cycling miles under your belt during the whole triathlon year. Beginners will do slightly less, and ambition and performance-oriented athletes more, according to their abilities. This means that cycling training is more time-consuming than the other disciplines. While you can complete your swimming and running workouts in one hour, much more than that is required for a cycling workout (except during the gentle regeneration sessions). This is why it is advisable to incorporate your training into your daily life, i.e., cycling to work, visiting friends by bike, going on bike rides with the family, etc.

Bike training differs greatly from one training phase to another. Let's start with the preparation phase:

8.4.1 First preparation phase (about two months)

Basic training

Basic endurance training builds special endurance. This means high volume training at low intensity. For a triathlon, this takes place in winter and in the first part of the preparation phase. This training can take place in the actual discipline (swimming, cycling or running), but this need not be the case. You can build your cycling base with long, gentle runs or cross-country skiing. Good basic endurance enables every triathlete to increase his training speed and mileage later in the season without the risk of overtraining.

Basic endurance training is primarily intended to improve aerobic endurance.

General aerobic endurance is characterized by working in steady-state conditions, so that the used muscle is guaranteed a sufficient supply of oxygen during a dynamic load.

This basic endurance training should be performed in a zone in which **60-75% of the HRmax** is attained by corresponding to tempo levels T1-T3. Cycling distances for Ironman 70.3 endurance training range from 20 to 80 miles.

For example, for a 35-year-old with a maximum heart rate of 190, this means:

$$60\text{-}75\% \text{ of } 190 = 115\text{-}143.$$

Basic cycling training should therefore be performed with an average heart rate of somewhere between 115 and 143. As cycling heart rates are very dependent on the course profile and external conditions (such as wind), it is the average heart rate for the whole workout that is important.

Focus on cycling

If you were unable to cycle during the winter due to bad weather and have decided to attend on a one- or two-week warm-weather cycling training camp in the first preparation phase, you should bear the following points in mind:

www.royhinnen.ch

Before you go, you should take every possible opportunity to cycle at least a couple of hundred miles per week. This is the only way to guarantee that you get the most benefits from the high-volume endurance training performed during the warm-weather training camp.

This important training phase lays the foundations for subsequent training. Long, gentle rides lasting up to several hours mainly serve to improve endurance and train your metabolism. You should stick to low gears and pedaling rates between 100 and 110 rpm and ride uphill in low gears sitting in the saddle as much as possible. If you ride out of the saddle, you are mainly using your strength to get up the hill, so that activity actually becomes strength endurance training instead of a basic endurance training activity.

We would like to warn you that even a training ride that was intended to be gentle may turn into a race, often leading to complete exhaustion, so that after 6 or 7 days at the most, you are completely burned out. In the second week, you will not be able to train every day because you will start to get injured and the remainder of your training camp will be wasted. To help prevent this, make sure to get enough rest.

The training goal must be to be able to train normally even on the last day of the training camp. Training should be constructive not destructive.

Here is a possible bike training camp schedule for an ambitious or performance-oriented athlete:

Day	Training
1	2 hours cycling, T2/50 mins. Swimming
2	3 hours cycling, T3/40 mins fartlek running
3	Regeneration/40 mins swimming
4	3 hours cycling T2/30 mins swimming, T3

5	4 hours cycling, T3/50 min. swim
6	5 hours cycling, T2-T3
7	Regeneration
8	3 hours cycling, T3/1:15 h fartlek run
9	4 hours cycling, T3/45 min swim
10	5 hour cycling, T2/T3
11	Regeneration / possibly 50 min swim
12	3 hours cycling, T3 + 1 hour run T2 ("brick" transition training)
13	Mountain ride 5-6 hours You should also include 15 minutes of stretching exercises every day and strengthening exercises three times per week

Fig. 19: Training schedule for a 14-day training camp.

Suitable terrain should be slightly hilly, particularly for the first training week. Short fartleks or a few rides between signposts could provide some variety among the long and gentle rides. The climbs in the second week should be ridden as much as possible in the saddle.

A specific training example (this one is Henry's) usually looks a little different, as the weather often requires changes to be made.

The objective of Henry's season was to participate in several Ironman 70.3 distances and in a full Ironman. Important benchmarks for a balanced training in this time are the morning resting heart rate, training sensation, and urea values. Urea is a metabolite of the protein metabolism and should not exceed a value of 55. Higher values are a sign of overtraining.

The starting plan should be: mid-March 350 miles cycling and a weekly mileage between 20 and 35 miles, plus 1-2 hours swimming training per week.

The training location was the Spanish island of Mallorca and rides were regularly performed in groups.

This information includes everything except the 45-minute stretching or core stability exercises performed on alternate days.

Day	Training	Resting pulse	Urea
1	1.5 hr bike, 30 min. swim in 25 yard pool	46	
2	4.5 hr bike, T3		
3	4 hr bike, T3/T4		45
4	5 hr bike, T2/T3	49	
5	Regeneration; 30 min swim, 1 hr run, T2	50	37
6	5 hr bike, T3	49	
7	6 hr bike, T2, hilly	50	39
8	Regeneration	52	
9	9 hr bike, at an altitude of 9200 ft., T2-T4	49	46
10	Regeneration, rest necessary	52	
11	3.5 hrs bike, T3 + 1 hr run, T2	51	41
12	(rain) 1 hr swim, partly with and without Neoprene	49	
13	3 hr bike, 40 min. swim	50	46
14	7 hr bike, T3	51	
15	Departure, "quite enough, 54 hrs in two weeks is the maximum"	53	54.9

Fig. 20: Henry's training plan for a 14-day training camp.

He completed a total of 760 miles on the bike, only 19 miles running and 3.5 miles swimming in 15 days. 54 training hours in two weeks represent maximal training for Henry. Average cycling speeds were 14 – 16 mph, which for Henry represent T2-T3, sometimes T4. The heart rates for cycling training lay between 115 and 125. The urea values, which were taken on an empty stomach every 2 days, were good at levels between 37 and 46. The value was a little high at 54.9 only after the last training day of 117 miles.

Another way of constructing a cycling block is to perform very long but gentle bike rides on weekends or days off. Doing three very long bike rides over three or four weekends is a good way of boosting your basic bike training.

For example:

- 31 miles/50 miles/37 miles
- 37 miles/56 miles/44 miles
- 44 miles/62 miles/50 miles
- 37 miles/74 miles/50 miles

which gives the following in terms of hours:

2	3	2.5
2.5	3.5	3
3	4	3
2.5	5	3

This will give you a good endurance base for the coming season.

8.4.2 Second preparation phase

In April, you can add the occasional higher intensity workout. However, training mostly consists of gentle bike rides as before. You should do bike speed work once a week. Below are four possible variations:

If you still find the following core workouts too intensive, you can add the following variants once a week.

Load intensities 1 x per week:

Variant	Warm-up	Load	Recovery	Repetitions	Cool-down
1	20-30 min.	20 min. T5	10 min T2	2-3 x	20-30 min
2	20-30 min	15 min T5	10 min T2	3-4 x	20-30 min
3	20-30 min	10 min T5	10 min T2	5-6 x	20-30 min
4	20-30 min	10 min T5	8 min T2	5-6 x	20-30 min

8.4.3 Competition phase from May onward

Continue to perform endurance rides as before. The faster sections of your core workouts are now performed in higher gears in order to become familiar with race pace. It is always important to hold back on speed after the quick sections. Interval training boosts endurance performance as a whole and at the same time improves cycling technique.

J. Bollwein

Interval training

Interval training on the bike should consist of three separate components: A warm-up, intervals and a final cool-down.

The simplest way of getting quick and relaxed pace training mileage under your belt is by doing fartlek training. Take what you learned in running and now apply it to cycling. Henry also likes to call this method "child's play," because it involves moving like children do. They move slowly, then suddenly fast, and then return to a leisurely pace. If we do this on the bike a few times, making the fast sections longer, or shorter according to our preference or how we feel. The only important thing is that the pace during the relaxed phases is really kept relaxed. So, after a 15-20 minute warm-up, increase your speed until you reach a preset goal, such as the next city limit sign, tower, etc. Repeat this little game 2-3 times or even 4-5 times. For a group training ride in which a few sprints are planned, we recommend racing between city limits signs.

For the last 12 weeks before the Ironman 70.3, we would recommend the following 12 core bike workouts, which are intended to improve race-specific endurance.

We have a few simple tips to increase your motivation for these tempo rides during training: You can take advantage of a tailwind, a partly downhill route, or the slipstream of a small group in order to familiarize yourself with the new, higher speeds.

8.4.4 The 12 core bike workouts

T7-race pace over 25 miles (Olympic Distance)
T6-race pace over 56 miles (Ironman 70.3)

Weeks	Distances	Explanations
1	12 miles, T5	Individual time trial (in regeneration week)
2	6 x 3 miles, T7	Even pace, rest every 3 miles
3	4 x 6 miles, T7	Increase second half, rest every 3 miles, relaxed
4	28 miles, T6	Even
5		Regeneration, relaxed cycling, T3
6	8 x 6 miles, T6	Rest every 2.5 miles, gentle pedaling
7	3 x 20 miles, T6	Rest every 3 miles, gentle pedaling
8	28 miles, T6/T7	
9		Regeneration, relaxed cycling, T3
10	8 x 6 miles, T6	Rest every 2 miles, gentle pedaling
11	6 x 9 miles, T6	Rest every 2.5 miles, gentle pedaling
12	28 miles, T6	
IM 70.3 week	Optional	

Fig. 21: Core bike workouts.

In addition, once a week, perform a relaxed, even-paced T3 50-80 mile bike ride. Include more bike training in the form of bike-run transition training.

Important! The cycling speed in the Ironman 70.3 (T6) is significantly higher than the average training speed.

For example: Race pace is 21.7 mph over 56 miles, while the average training speed is only 16.7-18.6 mph.

8.4.5 Extra cycling training tips

Strength endurance
Strength endurance is an important factor in cycling. It can be trained either by cycling for long distances uphill riding out of the saddle, or on the flat using a high gear and a low pedaling rate of only 60 rpm. One strength endurance workout per week should be incorporated into your training plan.

Cycling up long hills
Numerous triathletes, mainly from flat regions, struggle when it comes to long uphill climbs in competitions. Henry, who lives in an absolutely flat region has noticed that even very strong cyclists experience real anxiety when they have to ride in a hilly region nearby. It is not because they lack strength; it is rather a mental issue that needs to be overcome.

Anyone who entertains negative thoughts like: "I can't do it. This is agony. I hate this incline," should not be surprised if he struggles up every hill.

Henry's tip: Enjoy the fantastic views, take a close look at the wonders of nature and build confidence as you ride back downhill again. Say to yourself: "Ok mountain, I can deal with you, I am going to eat you for breakfast, I can do it, after all I can change gears." With this positive attitude, and the right pedaling rate, you can deal with any climb however long or steep.

Aerodynamics on the bike
First, a physical fact that nobody can escape or reason away:

Air resistance doubles with speed. Good aerodynamics reduce air resistance considerably, but it is not enough to possess a state-of-the-art, super-expensive racing bike and then neglect all other factors.

Bear the following points in mind:

- In training, try to find your optimal sitting position.

- Wear tight-fitting cycling clothes.

- The knees should be kept close to the top tube and parallel to the frame.

- Support your forearms on the aero handlebars for as long as possible.

- Keep your upper body still. The upper body starts to sway if your gear is too high.

Feeling comfortable on the bike
It is vital that you feel comfortable on the bike. To maintain an aerodynamic line throughout the whole 56 miles, you must also feel comfortable during this two- to three-hour period. In order to attain the right position, you need to do some fine tuning. This starts with the position of the aero handlebars (horizontal, tilted down or up) and saddle position, and continues to the position of the arm pads right up to the seat tube angle of the bike. All of this needs to be adapted to your individual circumstances. Long bike rides are a good opportunity to do this. You should experiment as you go along in order to attain the correct position.

8.4.6 Cycling training during transition phase

It would be ideal if you could keep your cycling going during the transition phase, in the months of October to February. In many regions, this is only possible on the dreaded bicycle roller or the odd weekend ride. Many triathletes therefore choose a different solution. They just drop cycling altogether during the cold, unpleasant season and stick to swimming and running.

However, if you are able to do the odd bike tour during this long regeneration phase, forget about speed and ride without any pressure. The aim should be gentle pedaling. During this period, mountain biking is a great, fun form of endurance training. There is also room for other alternatives such as cross-country skiing, etc.

8.4.7 Additional cycling tips

- For longer training rides, make sure you have plenty to drink and eat.
- Change gear at the right time when climbing hills and enjoy the experience of being on the incline and the descent.
- Always bring something to eat to prevent the dreaded depletion of the body's glycogen reserves.
- Always warm up and cool down for 15-20 minutes for interval training.
- Attack several bottle racks to your bike; take along a drink system.
- In cold weather, watch out for the wind chill factor.
- Always wear a helmet.
- Take spare inner tubes and a mini repair kit with you.
- The first six weeks in the preparation phase, only ride in low gears.
- First increase the training volume, then the intensity.
- On one training day, strength training can follow and an endurance workout, but not vice versa.
- Make sure you always maintain a regeneration week.

Photo: Bakke-Svensson/WTC

8.5 Improve your running

Running, the final element of the race, is for many triathletes the hardest discipline in the non-stop endurance triathlon. Running training may be arduous for many, but it offers many benefits. Without spending much money, we can run any time and any place. Another benefit of running is the fact that this discipline can be practiced in any weather, with the exception of thunderstorms, at any time of day and year and in any surroundings. Unlike cycling, you can run regularly in the dark, rain and snow of the fall and winter months.

If you can start running directly from home, you will save traveling time. In addition, running is the most energy-intensive of the three triathlon disciplines. During the cold months, it may be advisable to run instead of cycle. One hour of running training is more effective than 1-2 hours worth of cycling, where you would also run the risk of getting cold. Hill runs also develop strength for cycling.

Photo: Bakke-Svensson/WTC

Running style

Make as few changes to your running style as possible, especially if you have no injuries. It is very easy to read about optimal running style, but it is difficult to copy something predefined. If you have been running with the same style for 20, 30, 40, 50 years, or even longer, then don't change it. Changing your running style can lead to injury, as the body is forced to adopt an unfamiliar posture. It also takes a very, very long time to shake off old habits, as you likely learned these movements early in your training. Marlies has already heard many people say how "badly" she runs, but as she has had no problems with her running style up to now, she has not changed it very much. It is worth mentioning in passing that Marlies can run a 2:45:08h marathon.

Our tip:

Run as economically as possible and without using too much strength!

Breathing

Many athletes try to breathe as quietly as possible. This makes the breathing very flat and shallow. This quiet breathing often began in our school days, when we didn't want to show our rivals that we were trying too hard. But it is very important to breathe deliberately to eliminate the "used" air from our bodies.

Our tip:

Actively breathe in and out, making particularly sure that you breathe out deliberately!

After the gentle training of the transition period, a sensible running training structure can look as follows:

Basic endurance training	2-3 months
Endurance + speed endurance training	6 weeks
Endurance and interval training	6 weeks

8.5.1 Basic endurance training

Basic endurance training takes place in the aerobic zone, or in **steady state**. This term refers to the oxygen balance, which means that you take in only as much oxygen as is necessary to supply your energy. Basic endurance training should be performed in such a way that you can chat easily with others. It constitutes 65-75% of maximal performance (T1-T3).

In this kind of training, you must constantly have the feeling that you could run faster. Overall, your all-round condition will improve. This is achieved by longer workouts, particularly long, gentle and steady runs. Hard training at this time does more harm than good.

In this two- or three-month period, many miles should be run in the aerobic zone. Competitive triathletes can compete in fun runs for variety; don't run flat out though, just run as you would in training. Short, once-a-week fartleks also add variety.

For training blocks focusing on one discipline, the training volume is either kept the same or increased only gradually.

Block training in the basic endurance training schedule

Below is a specific example of a running training block, based on basic training of approximately 20 miles per week, divided into 2-3 separate sessions. Blocked training lasts for a period of 3-4 weeks (January or February), when the training frequency is increased from 2 or 3 to 4 sessions.

Example: Basic training 21.7 miles

Week 1: Increase to 28 miles

Frequency	Training Volume	Description
1x	5 miles	Relaxed, T3, with short fartlek T5
2x	7 miles	Gentle, T2
1x	9 miles	Slow, T1

Week 2: Increase to 31 miles

Frequency	Training Volume	Description
1x	8 miles	Relaxed with 3 quick sections, T5
2x	6 miles	Gentle, T2
1x	9 miles	Relaxed, T3

Week 3: Increase to 37 miles

Frequency	Training Volume	Description
1x	8 miles	Relaxed with 3 quick sections, T5
2x	9 miles	Gentle, T2
1x	11 miles	Relaxed, T3

Possible Week 4: Total volume 44 miles

Frequency	Training Volume	Description
1x	8 miles	T3, with fartlek, T5
2x	11 miles	Relaxed, T3
1x	14 miles	Gentle, T2

Fig. 23: Training blocks.

This running block is followed by a regeneration week of two-mile recreational runs.

If your weekly mileage is only 15 miles, it will increase to 22 miles, 28 miles, 32 miles and then 37 miles. This is then followed by a real regeneration week with only 2 x 5 mile recreational runs.

Step-shaped basic training structure

A step-shaped structure in the preparation phase can also be an alternative to a training block.

Four possibilities of basic endurance are outlined in the chart below. The volumes are shown in miles per week for each. Regeneration weeks are labeled "reg."

Week	Volume in miles	Alternative 1	Alternative 2	Alternative 3	My training
1	19	25	25	15	
2	22	28	28	18	
3	25	31	14 reg.	12 reg.	
4	12 reg.	16 reg.	28	18	
5	19	31	31	22	
6	28	34	15	12 reg.	
7	28	38	31	20	

Week	Volume in miles	Alternative 1	Alternative 2	Alternative 3	My training
8	14 reg.	19 reg.	34	25	
9	22	31	17 reg.	12 reg.	
10	28	38	34	25	
11	31	43	37	28	
12	15 reg.	22 reg.	18 reg.	14 reg.	

Fig. 24: Step-shaped training structure.

A regeneration week should take place after at least three weeks with only 60% volume and reduced intensity. Triathletes in their 40s or 50s, and those with significant professional or family commitments, should add another regeneration week after the second training week.

M. Meyer

8.5.2   Speed endurance training

As well as a good basic endurance foundation, speed and strength workouts are also required to improve your running performance. These include longer fartlek workouts, hill running, tempo endurance runs and interval runs. But be careful: These intensive runs must also be preceded and followed by relaxed endurance sessions. The ratio of these fast miles in the competition period should not account for more than 20-25% of the running volume, depending on the athlete's ability. You should build up gradually to this limit. Finally, quick cycling and swimming workouts should also be included.

Speed endurance training starts with 4-5 **hill runs** (300-700 yards quick, T5 uphill), and can be increased by 1 run every week.

Fartlek as a short tempo endurance run
During a run, accelerate up to the next house, the end of the woods, the next tree, or any other landmark you choose. This quick section is followed by gentle jogging or trotting until

you recover. When you recover, start the little game over. It is up to you to determine the speed. Fartlek is intensive, flexible and has no predefined distances or tempos. The triathlete runs exactly as fast as he or she wants. Fartlek is playful and creative tempo work. It also has the great advantage that these fun versions need no pre-measured distances or 4,000 yard track.

After the fartlek workout, do some relaxed jogging and light stretching.

Tempo endurance run
- 15-25 min, 5-10 sec below 10K race tempo, with warm-up and cool-down jog

If you are coping well with the training, the times can be extended by a few minutes.

These runs improve speed endurance, and it is a good idea to insert one after a relaxed bike workout of 12-18 miles in the form of "brick" training.

Interval training
Ambitious and performance-oriented triathletes use interval training to boost their running speed. But be careful, at the first signs of overtraining, interval training should be replaced by very gentle endurance training. Interval training enables us to improve our speed and thereby our performance. We not only develop our speed, strength and motor skills, but also our willpower.

For a medium distance triathlon, suitable intervals are from 1,100 to 3,300 yards in the following form (of course, don't forget to warm up and cool down).

- 6-8 x 1,000 yards at 10k race pace, jog rest 1,000 yards until pulse < 110

- 3-4 x 2,000 yards, 5-10 s below 10K race pace, jog rest 2,000 yards until pulse < 110

- 2-3 x 3,000 yards, 10-15 s below 10K race pace, jog rest 2,000 yards until pulse < 110

Interval training is usually carried out on a 400-yard track, but measured distances on a road or country lane are equally suitable. This applies to people who do not live near a running track or who just don't like running on a cinder or tartan track.

8.5.3 Competition running intensities

Distance	% of HRmax when running (approx.)
5km	100
10km	95
13.1 miles	Half Marathon 90
26.2 miles	Marathon 85-88

Fig. 25: Race intensities (running).

8.5.4 Half marathon time calculator

The table below shows possible half marathon times based on known 10 km times:

Actual 10 km time in minutes	Corresponds to 1,000 m time in minutes	Possible half marathon time in hours
35	3:30	1:18
36	3:36	1:20
37	3:42	1:22
38	3:48	1:24
39	3:54	1:27
40	4:00	1:29
41	4:06	1:31
42	4:12	1:33
43	4:18	1:36
44	4:24	1:38
45	4:30	1:40
46	4:36	1:42
47	4:42	1:44
48	4:48	1:47
49	4:54	1:49
50	5:00	1:51
51	5:06	1:53
52	5:12	1:56
53	5:18	1:58
54	5:24	2:00
55	5:30	2:02
56	5:36	2:04
57	5:42	2:07
58	5:48	2:09
59	5:54	2:11
60	6:00	2:13

Fig. 26: Possible half marathon times based on actual 10km times.

The values are based on the following calculation:
half marathon time = 10 km time x 2.222

What is the difference between a **"solo half marathon time"** and an **"Ironman 70.3 half marathon time"**?

- **For good runners, approximately 8-10 minutes**
- **For average runners approximately 15 minutes**

8.5.5 The 12 core running workouts

	Distances	Explanations
1	2 hrs	Endurance, T3
2	6 x 500-800 yards	Hill training 6 x 600 yards, or longer fartlek
3	15-25 min	Tempo endurance run, T5-T6
4	10 km	Fun run, 10 km race pace T7
5	2 hr	Relaxed run, T3
6	6 x 1,000 yards	10 km pace, T7, recovery 5 min, T2, gentle
7	3 x 4,000 yards	Solo half marathon pace, Jog 2200 yards recovery
8	15 km	10 s. faster per km than IM half marathon pace
9	2 hrs	Relaxed run, T3
10	8 x 1,000 yards	1000 m sections at 10km pace, T7, recovery every 5 min, T2 gentle
11	3 x 5km	10 s. faster than solo half marathon pace, recovery 2200 yards jogging
12	18 km	10 s. faster per km than IM half marathon pace
IM 70.3 week	Optional	4 days before Ironman 70.3: Glycogen training 2.5-3 mile run (T6-T7) + 6 mile bike (T6)

Fig. 27: Core running workouts.

8.5.6 Additional running tips

- Incorporate running drills into your training once a week.
- Alternate several pairs of running shoes.

- Structure your workouts as follows: Approximately 10 mins warm-up or jog, endurance training followed by cool-down and stretching.
- Treat all chafed areas with a little grease or Vaseline.
- Clothing should be tight-fitting but not restrict movement.
- In runs of two hours or more, practice drinking plenty of fluids.
- In cold weather, it is better to wear several thin layers of clothing than a few thick layers.
- Within your training group, correct each others' running style.
- Enjoy your training.
- It is better to reduce or even completely drop a workout than to force yourself to train when you don't want to.

Skinfit

8.6 Strength endurance training

Optimal technique and strength are required if you want to swim, cycle and run with apparent ease as Jan Sibbersen, Normann Stadler and Timo Bracht do. A crucial factor for outstanding technique in all three disciplines is core stability (strong abdominal and back muscles). With technique and strength, we can protect ourselves from injuries and also save ourselves some training mileage. For this reason, regular strengthening and core stability exercises belong in every triathlete's training plan. Strength endurance training can easily be incorporated into normal technique and speed training.

Sport	Technique Training	Strength Endurance Training
Swimming	Training with kickboard and pull buoy, one-armed crawl, high elbows with clenched fist, outstretched fingers, etc.	Swimming with paddles, swimming with t-shirt, pair-work swimming exercises
Cycling	One-legged pedaling, curve cycling, cycling uphill	Hill intervals, intervals on the flat with high gears and pedaling rate of 60 rpm
Running	Running drills, cross-country runs	Hill runs, short acceleration runs (e.g. 3 x 200 yds) after long endurance runs

Fig. 28: Strength endurance training.

8.7 Reducing transition times

The first triathlon transition from swimming to cycling is primarily a matter of organization. Preparation with military precision is very helpful and saves a lot of time. Use a swimming workout in the lake as an opportunity to practice the swim/bike transition. You can read more about this in chapter 10, "Race Week." This transition does not present any muscular problems, unlike the second bike/run transition. You must practice this second transition regularly in order to get used to the heavy feeling in your legs and the time it takes to get into your running rhythm, which slows you down.

Our Tip: In the last mile of the cycling course, deliberately reduce the pressure on the pedals and relaxe the muscles by increasing your pedaling rate.

Transition or brick training can be structured as follows:
• Long, relaxed endurance bike ride directly followed by a short, quick run (e.g., 50 mile bike ride, T3 + 2 mile run, quick, T5, or 30 miles bike, T3 + 4 mile run, quick, T5).
• Short, quick training bike ride directly followed by a long, slow run (e.g., 25 mile bike ride, quick, T5 + 6-11 mile run, relaxed, T2-T3).

M. Meyer

9 Performance Testing and Self-Motivation

For every triathlete – particularly for ambitious and performance-oriented athletes – self-motivation can sometimes be a problem. Dragging oneself out of a comfortable house in wet or windy weather requires a great deal of willpower and real motivation. There are many methods and tricks to help you develop and even strengthen this throughout the year.

If we understand why we do triathlons, the "how" should not be an issue. The answers to the question "Why do we do triathlons?" are many and differ greatly from one person to another.

So while some triathletes are content "just" to meet their self-set challenge, (i.e., finishing regardless of the time), others are motivated by such factors as:

- Finding their own limits
- Setting a personal record
- Setting a club record
- Finishing first in their age group
- Beating a long-standing rival
- Setting a district, regional or national record, etc.

Other motivations may be:

Health reasons: weight loss, improving one's figure, establishing greater well-being, aging healthily, etc.
Social reasons: the fun of group training, shared experiences, greater self-confidence, meaningful activity, etc.

Despite your best intentions, the above-mentioned arguments can nix your planned workout if you lack the necessary motivation and willpower.

9.1 Self-motivation

Motivation is what encourages us to keep going when the going gets tough. This can happen by:

- Having pride in your achievements (Olympic triathlon, half marathon time, 2,000 yards swimming, reduced BMI, weight loss, improved sporting performance, great press reports, record run, victory, prize money etc.).
- Admiring other athletes as positive role models without envying their success.
- Visualizing how great it would be to be really fit and have even more strength, fun and success.

You must use your own individual environment as a starting point for your success and not be distracted by the fact that a club mate may have better circumstances than you. Your success is based on your foundations, not other people's.

Improve motivation:

- Make exercise fun.
- Take an interest in the natural world around you.
- Don't forget why you want to practice sports in the first place, whether it's to improve your figure, improve performance, strengthen your immune system, strengthen your heart and musculature, improve your well-being, etc.

Do not forget to:

- **Vary training**

- **Find new challenges for a new season**

- **Enjoy group training**

- **Train to music or in complete silence**

- **Set realistic goals**

- **Keep a training log**

- **Monitor performance**

Let us go into a little more detail concerning the last seven points:

Vary training

For triathletes, basic endurance training is the foundation for both improved health and competition-specific training. Increase your motivation by varying your training. In practical triathlon terms, this can mean during basic endurance training running, swimming and cycling only once a week, but doing another two workouts, e.g., inline skating, hiking, strength training or cross-country skiing.

Find new challenges for the new season

If you have been doing the same competitions for years, it will be motivating to find new challenges. Doing something different is exciting in itself. What about an Ironman 70.3 or even a full Ironman? Or a triathlon with an unusual cycling or running course? Perhaps en route to your vacation destination, you make a side trip for a mountain run, or a cross-country marathon – why should you only stick to flat tarmac? Go mountain biking in the forest or swim across a lake or a triathlon somewhere different. Every year, new sporting challenges do pop up, and they are easy to find in specialist triathlon publications.

Enjoy group training

Many triathletes find that regular group training motivates them. Exercising with others is fun and makes the workout goes more quickly. Look for training groups inside and outside your club. Take the initiative to invite friends, acquaintances or work colleagues.

Train to music or in complete silence

Not all triathletes like group training. The fact that we have no time constraints and can train alone means that we can listen to our favorite music or just "let ourselves go" and relax. This can have great effects. Phases of relaxation encourage creativity because the blood supply to the right half of the brain increases during moderate exercise. It was just this aspect that encouraged Henry to take up endurance sports 30 years ago. He was able to solve countless scientific problems while running. The other positives only came later (improved fitness, well-being, athletic ambition, etc.).

©Bakke-Svensson/WTC

Set realistic goals

It is a good idea to divide your goal of being an Ironman 70.3 finisher into partial goals, so it is "step-by-step." The first steps could be:

An Olympic triathlon, cycling 62 miles or running a half marathon.

Other athletic goals could include: completing an Ironman 70.3 in 5:59, running a 10K in 40 minutes, a marathon in 3:59, swimming across a lake, losing weight, reducing body fat or just getting faster.

It is easier to train toward such speciffic goals than toward vague or unrealistic target times.

Several factors influence our training and these should be kept in mind when setting realistic goals: Age, ability, state of health, available time and willpower.

As far as **age** is concerned, we now know that there are no constraints for endurance sports success. Even people over 70 can still workout and can improve their fitness by means of regular, moderate endurance training. There are numerous positive examples at triathlon events.

Talent is what we were born with – or perhaps not – as the case may be! But talent alone is not enough to guarantee success. You also need regular training, discipline, willpower and the right attitude. Fortunately, the less talented among us can have just as much fun and success in their athletic endeavors by being realistic about their potential.

Your **health** should be checked at least once a year by a physician.

Time is a problematic issue for many busy people. Luckily, there are 24 hours in every day, so you should be able to find time to incorporate your training into your daily routine. If you watch TV for 25 hours a week (the average in the U.S.), it should not be too hard to carry out a few hours training per week. After all, there are 168 hours in every week. People who claim to have no time to exercise often have to spend several hours in the physician's waiting room later.

Another example to illustrate this tricky time issue is the top manager who works 13-15 hours a day and admittedly has little time for sports. However, he is able to suddenly find time to spend with a new girlfriend. We should therefore treat our sport as we would a new boyfriend or girlfriend!

Willpower is required in order to actually accomplish your objectives. This is not only true for sports, either. If you train your willpower by exercising regularly, you will be able to transfer this ability into your private and professional life.

Keep a training log

Keeping a training log gives you a reassuring feeling, like having money in the bank. Every movement represents an asset that provides annual interest in the form of improved fitness. A training log also helps you spot training errors and avoid repeating them. It is not only important to record your training volume, but also the intensity, T1-T8. You should measure your resting heart rate and weight at exactly the same time each day, it is best to weigh yourself after you wake up in the morning, and take your resting heart rate before you get up. Under comments, you should write down everything that is or could be important, such as weather conditions for the day, hills, new shoes, a late night, birthday party, tired legs, stiff arms, not in the mood for training. etc.

Write down the comments so you are constantly reminded of them.

If your training log is still empty on Friday, for example, you still have the weekend to make up for lost time. But if you suddenly increase your weekly training, you will be able to see this immediately by looking at the total training times. Give yourself a pat on the back if you have reached or exceeded a certain goal you should be proud of yourself.

9.2 Performance testing methods

Monitoring one's own performance can be a great source of motivation for triathletes, particularly if this involves simple methods of checking our training progression or regression (in the case of overtraining). So what are these simple measures?

Without any great financial outlay, we can carry out the following six procedures ourselves from time to time, e.g., at 4-6 week intervals. Just as a note, medical assistance is required for the seventh method. Don't forget to make a note of these figures in your training log!

1. Attitude
2. Heart rate
3. BMI values
4. Reduction in body fat
5. Cooper endurance test
6. Improved competition times
7. Exercise ECG test at sports clinic

9.2.1 Attitude

From time to time, make a note of how you feel when exercising, e.g., no improvement, slight improvement, distinct improvement. Also write down your daily feelings, such as light, relaxed, lazy, slow, great. It can often be very helpful to look back on these comments if you get an infection or feel better and stronger from month to month.

9.2.2 Heart rate

Measure your resting heart rate once a week before getting up. If it drops a little, you are on the right track. If your training heart rate at the same speed over the same distance also drops, your form is clearly improving. You are on the road to success. However, if your resting heart rate is more than 6-8 bpm faster than normal, stop training, because an infection or illness is on its way. If it rises by 5bpm, you have trained too hard the previous days, so you should train more gently and for less time. Instead of running for one hour, just go for a gentle 30 minute jog.

9.2.3 BMI values

The Body Mass Index (BMI) tells us a lot about our bodyweight. It is calculated by dividing the bodyweight in lbs, by the square of the body height in inches, then multiplying the total by 703.

BMI = (Weight in lbs / height in inches squared) x 703

An example: Bodyweight 177 lbs divided by height 74 inches.
BMI = $177/74^2$ = 22.5.

M. Nüsken

More Examples of calculated BMI Values:

Bodyweight in lbs	Height in inches	Height squared in lbs/ height	BMI = bodyweight squared
130	63	3969	23.03
130	67	4489	20.36
155	67	4489	24.27
155	74	5476	19.9
175	71	5041	24.41
175	73	5329	23.09
175	75	5625	21.87
190	69	4761	28.05

Fig. 29: BMI values.

BMI Guidelines:

	Women	Men
Underweight	‹ 19	‹ 20
Normal weight	19-24	20-25
Overweight	24-30	25-30
Obese	› 30	› 30

Fig. 30: BMI Guidelines.

It's easy to see your own level. If your BMI level drops, your body becomes fitter and more toned. For underweight people, exercise and a good diet will cause the BMI to increase, i.e., to normalize.

However, the BMI gives us little indication of the personal body fat ratio though, and body fat percentage is another interesting value that should be measured in a separate process.

9.2.4 Reduction of body fat percentage

The easiest way to measure body fat percentage is using bodyfat scales. As this value is often very inaccurate, you should weigh yourself in a pharmacy. Henry's body-fat scales for example show values of 20-24%, whereas different scales give values between 17% and only 6%.

For the purposes of comparison, you should always use the same scales.

In the evaluation of body fat as a percentage, the following values are applicable depending on age:

Women:

Age	Very Good	Good	Average	Bad
20-24	18.9	22.1	25.0	29.6
25-29	19.9	22.0	25.4	29.8
30-34	19.7	22.7	26.4	30.6
35-39	21.0	24.0	27.7	31.5
40-44	22.6	25.6	29.3	32.8
45-49	24.3	27.3	30.9	34.1
50-59	26.6	29.7	33.1	36.2
60+	27.4	30.7	34.0	37.2

Men:

Age	Very Good	Good	Average	Bad
20-24	18.9	14.9	19.0	23.3
25-29	12.8	16.5	20.3	24.3
30-34	14.5	18.0	21.5	25.2
35-39	16.1	19.3	22.6	26.1
40-44	17.5	20.5	23.6	26.9
45-49	18.6	21.5	24.5	27.6
50-59	18.6	21.5	24.5	27.6
60+	20.2	23.2	26.2	29.3

Fig. 31: Body Fat Percentage Chart.

The body fat percentage increases with age. Because of biological reasons, conditioning, the human body naturally lays down bigger reserves in case hard times are ahead.

9.2.5 Cooper endurance test

Out of all the various practical tests that can be performed without great difficulty, the so-called Cooper Test has proven to be the best. This running test – developed by American Sports Physician and astronaut Dr. Kenneth Cooper – is best performed on a fat 440-yard running track, as the distance covered in 12 minutes constitutes a measurement of running ability. If you don't have professional running track available, this test can be carried out on a country road. An automobile traveling behind the runner beeps its horn at the start and finish and measures the distance covered with the odometer.

The greater the distance covered, the better your running form. Due to their reduced muscle mass, women are not able to run as far as men in the same fitness category.

Results in miles according to age

Fitness Category	Gender	13-19 years	20-29 years	30-39 years	40-49 years	50-59 years	60+ years
I. Very weak	Men	‹1.29	‹1.20	‹1.17	‹1.13	‹1.03	‹0.84
	Women	‹1.00	‹0.90	‹0.93	‹0.88	‹0.83	‹0.78
II. Weak	Men	1.29-1.36	1.2-1.3	1.17-1.29	1.13-1.23	1.03-1.16	0.86-1.01
	Women	1-1.17	0.96-1.11	0.95-1.04	0.88-0.98	0.83-0.93	0.78-0.86
III. Average	Men	1.37-1.55	1.31-1.48	1.30-1.44	1.24-1.39	1.16-1.29	1.03-1.19
	Women	1.18-1.28	1.11-1.20	1.06-1.17	0.98-1.11	0.93-1.04	0.86-0.98
IV. Good	Men	1.56-1.71	1.49-1.63	1.45-1.55	1.39-1.52	1.30-1.43	1.21-1.31
	Women	1.29-1.42	1.22-1.33	1.18-1.28	1.11-1.23	1.06-1.17	0.98-1.08
V. Very good	Men	1.72-1.85	1.64-1.75	1.56-1.68	1.53-1.64	1.44-1.57	1.32-1.54
	Women	1.43-1.50	1.34-1.44	1.29-1.38	1.24-1.33	1.18-1.29	1.09-1.17
VI. Excellent	Men	›1.86	›1.86	›1.69	›1.65	›1.58	›1.55
	Women	›1.51	›1.45	›1.39	›1.34	›1.30	›1.18

Figure 32: Cooper Test – performance tables.

(source: Cooper, 1994: *Dr. Cooper Health Program. Movement, Nutrition, Mental Balance.* Droemer)

This 12-minute test is not only a reliable gauge of fitness, but also provides reliable information concerning **running progress and thereby reinforces personal motivation**. As this test can be conducted without outside assistance and with no great financial outlay, you should use it to test your form every six weeks. You will be amazed at how much progress you can make if you train correctly.

A **tip** on how to carry out the test:

Try to carry out the test in pairs, threes or in a group. It is easier to run like this than alone.

9.2.6 Improving race times

If the time you take to run a certain distance or triathlon is reduced, it means your performance has improved. This helps motivate triathletes better than most other ways. This definitely includes Marlies, who is a bona-fide competitor and takes part in 20 races or more every year. Naturally, Marlies only pushes herself to the limit in a few races (peaks); she uses many races as hard workouts.

9.2.7 Exercise ECG test

An exercise electrocardiogram (ECG) test can either be performed on an exercise bike or treadmill. The blood pressure and working heart rate are recorded as the load is increased. As the test is performed under medical supervision, maximal loading is possible. Due to the costs incurred, it is advisable to discuss this aspect with a physician beforehand.

9.3 Performance testing advantages

Performance monitoring should definitely be carried out every 4-6 weeks and is always a good idea. The cost involved for the first six methods is low and can easily be incorporated into a normal training routine.

If the data shows fitness has improved:

- Improved confidence.
- Increased motivation.
- We reap the rewards for all our hard work.

If the data shows fitness has declined:

- This encourages us to look critically at our training and make changes to our training and/or nutrition.
- Now may be the time to set smaller (or even partial) goals in order to be able to obtain positive results in next month's test.

Bakke-Svensson/Ironman

10 Race Week

10.1 Nutrition

During race week, the issue of **nutrition** increases in importance.

The longer the distance, the more important your nutritional preparation should be. This is why we would like to give you some pointers on how to cope with the Ironman 70.3 course. The following two common problems should be avoided at all costs:
- Gastro intestinal problems
- The "bonk"

These problems can be avoided by experimenting with your race diet both in training and particularly in the test races. Unfortunately, there is no single formula that works for everyone.

Avoiding the "bonk"

The "bonk" is a term for the hypoglycemic attacks dreaded by cyclists. The symptoms are dizziness or cold sweats. The only solution here is to quickly consume digestible carbohydrates, which is why it is important to always take energy bars on long training rides.

Nutrition during race week

Ideally you should consume carbohydrates during race week as they provide considerably more effective energy than fats or protein. The goal is the optimal filling of the glycogen reserves according to the principle of supercompensation. If the Ironman 70.3 or medium distance is taking place on a Saturday, on the Tuesday before, deplete your glycogen reserves during the last hard workout (2-mile warm-up + 2.5-3.5 mile tempo run + 1.3 mile cool-down + 6.2 miles hard cycling training + 3 miles relaxed pedaling), and on Wednesday, Thursday and Friday focus on eating carbohydrates. This will significantly increase your glycogen reserves in the running and cycling muscles. If the Ironman 70.3 takes place on a Sunday, your glycogen-depletion training should take place on a Wednesday. Hard training is followed by recovery days.

H. Rauschmayr

On the days before the Ironman 70.3

- Eat 5-6 smaller meals evenly distributed throughout the day to place less stress on the digestive organs.
- Avoid gassy and hard-to-digest food! This includes beans, as well as raw greens, mayonnaise and wholegrain bread.
- Increase the carbohydrate ratio by limiting fats like sausage, meat, cheese, eggs. Watch out: Hidden fats are still fats!
- Ideally you should consume easily digestible food like potatoes, pasta, rice, cereal products.
- Drink copious amounts of water containing salt, juices, or tea.
- The urine should be clear or lightly colored.

The day before and the morning of the race

No more experimenting: From now on you should eat according to nutritional guidelines, eating foods such as fruit, vegetables, familiar wholegrain products and energy-rich carbohydrates. You can still eat normally in the evening. But this is not always easy because you often eat out after a long journey, such as a trip to Hawaii, or other competition locations.

On the day before the race you should ensure that you have answers to the following questions regarding the race itself:

- What is the course like? How many laps of the course are there?
- How many aid stations are there?
- What will be provided at each station?
- What and how much should I take with me for the cycling?
- Are personal helpers allowed? If so, where?
- What will the temperatures be like?

The morning of the race

Three to four hours before the race, the alarm clock goes off. For Henry, it's the worst moment of the day. It can happen as early as 4am. Most triathletes ask themselves: "Does it really have to be today?" Yes, it must, if you want to finish. You've wanted to do this for many months now. The pre-race breakfast consists of easily-digested food, bread (not wholegrain), marmalade, honey, yogurt with a little granola, coffee, tea and salted water. Henry's best experiences have been with kvass (a mildly alcoholic "bread drink" beverage made from fermented black or rye bread) + apple juice + water. Be careful with milk as this can lead to problems when combined with salty water. One hour before the start, drink $1/_2$ to 1 pint of fluids.

The race

The Ironman 70.3 can last between four and six hours, perhaps longer. Our body's energy reserves (glycogen) last 2-3 hours at most, meaning energy must be consumed during the race. If we assume about 1,000 kcal are burned per hour of competition, it is easy to calculate how much energy must be consumed and made available to the body during the race (the keyword is fatburning).

In general, there are two different processes you must prepare for where race nutrition is concerned:

1. The supply of easily digested energy by consuming carbohydrates.
2. The supply of electrolytes (minerals) for the metabolism and musculature, in order to prevent cramping.

Carbohydrates are a quick source of energy and can be consumed either in liquid or solid form. As the consumption of solids slows down digestion, it is imperative that your planned form of race nutrition be tested in training. Your body can utilize 2-2.5 ounces of carbohydrates per hour, and liquid carbohydrates can usually be converted more quickly and easily by the body than carbohydrates from solids. You should find out in training which type of carbohydrates suit you best.

2-2.5 ounces of liquid per hour should also be consumed, ideally in a concentration that does not exceed 8% (i.e., a maximum of 1.3 ounces per pint of liquid). This is important for triathletes who mix their drinks themselves. Salt should also be added. But 2-2.5 ounces per hour is a lot. If you don't like the taste of your gels or bars, you will soon prefer to go without and have a bad experience in the form of a "bonk" later in the running course.

Your gels and energy bars should fulfill the following requirements: They should taste good and be easily digestible. So it is essential to test them personally in advance!

However, be careful. One bar an hour is not nearly enough. A gel usually contains less than 1 ounce of carbohydrates, as do several energy bars. So in order to consume 2-2.5 ounces, you will have to eat three gels or bars, especially on the bike. As this is a lot, Henry uses a simple trick: For some time now, he has stuck a small slip of paper on his handlebar that shows the carbohydrate content per gel or bar. This note reminds him to consume energy during the cycling. There is always time to calculate this, and it should be emphasized that these carbohydrates should be consumed along with plenty of fluids.

Fluid intake

Lost **electrolytes** should be regularly replaced by consuming electrolyte drinks. These are placed at regular intervals along the cycling and running courses during every competition. You should start your fluid intake as soon as you get onto your bike.

The most important drink is, of course, **water. Not just tap water, but water with added salt.** When you sweat, you lose more than 0.03 ounces of salt per pint. This must be replaced to avoid risking low blood sodium levels (hyponatremia).

The sweat loss can – depending on weather conditions, humidity and course profile – be as much as 2-4 pints per hour. These must be replaced to avoid a drop in performance levels. In any case, it is advisable to fit a drink system to your handlebars, in which you can mix your drinks to suit yourself. We usually take one bottle of water for every bottle of electrolyte drink and mix them to suit our taste. The water is used to wash down the energy bars and gels and the electrolyte drinks are used for mineral balance.

Gels and solid energy bars are best digested when they are consumed with water or an electrolyte drink.

For more than 20 years, Henry has had success with his own mixture of Kvass + apple juice which he takes with him on the bike in two bottles. He has managed to stay completely cramp-free in both training and competition by taking alternate sips of water + mineral drink.

If energy bars and gels are too sweet for you, we suggest eating small pieces of bread to hide the taste.

On the running course, you no longer need to consume solid food, although cookies or even a piece of banana won't do any harm as they are very easy to digest. The intake of fluids is vital here though. As it is not possible to take your drinks with you – and is actually banned – you must take what is offered. Electrolyte drinks, water and cola are provided everywhere and can be mixed. As you have already learned, it is easier for the body to absorb a slightly electrolytic drink than pure water. Cola ensures a short-term rise in blood sugar levels. However, if the cola is taken at short, regular intervals, the blood sugar levels drop instead of rising, thus leading to a drop in performance.

In high temperatures, there is a way to reduce sweating and at the same time enjoy restorative refreshment. Just pour water over your head and neck or cool your arms and legs with water sponges. This dissipates excess heat and at the same time refreshes the overheated body. Covering your head, possibly with a damp cloth to cover the back of your neck, reinforces this positive effect.

T. Frahm

Important tips:
- Don't try out anything new or unfamiliar in a competition. Here you should stick to what is tried and tested, as you will have had plenty of time to determine what suits you during your long training sessions.
- Consume small amounts of carbohydrates and electrolytes at regular 10-15 minute intervals.
- On the bike, you should consume 2-2.5 ounces of carbohydrates in liquid or solid form. Your glycogen reserves should suffice for the swimming and running.
- In order to maintain physical performance levels (according to the Sports Institute of the University of Bayreuth, Germany) one pint of liquid should contain 0.01 – 0.028 ounces of sodium.
- Tap water should not be used to drink, but instead to cool your body down.
- As you also lose other minerals and trace elements other than sodium when you sweat, you should consume mineralized electrolyte drinks.
- Your body can absorb about 1.7 pints of liquid per hour.

If you try to complete the Ironman 70.3 without consuming any liquids or food, you will only reach the finish on a gurney or end up in the hospital!

10.2 The Big Day

Countdown to the Ironman 70.3

Weeks before:
- Test your equipment in preparation races.
- Practice drinking and eating during long cycling and running workouts.
- Set realistic target times (Plan A).
- Plan B for unexpected problems.
- Plan C is to just finish.
- Break in your running shoes!

Race week:
- Perform glycogen training on Tuesday if your triathlon takes place on a Saturday. Do it on Wednesday if the race is Sunday.
- Check your equipment, particularly the bike, brakes, steering head bearing, chain, pedals, etc.

The last three days:
- Drink a lot. Your urine should be clear.

The day before:
- Travel to the race, collect start documentation and, if possible, visit the cycling and running courses.
- Visit the swimming course, take note of landmarks as points of reference, and possibly swim through the course.
- Keep calm.
- Bear the weather forecast in mind when you prepare your clothing.
- It is essential to attend the race briefing!
- Pasta party – meet great people and see familiar faces. Awesome!
- Have I got everything ready? Put in my chip?
- You will probably be too nervous to get a good night's sleep, but it often helps to know that others are feeling the same way.

The big day
- Get up early, at least 3-4 hours before the start.
- Have an easily digestible breakfast, no granola, no milk, nothing heavy. You can drink coffee but follow it with plenty of liquids. Tip: Always carry a bottle of liquid with you.
- Set up your transition spot. It is better to prepare too much than not enough. Pump up your tires, put your bike in the correct gear, set up your cycling shoes. Is everything in its place? Set the bike computer to zero. Remember your glasses, starting number band, helmet, perhaps gloves, running shoes, cap, tights, cycling jersey, jacket, trousers, mini pump or CO_2 cartridge, liquid and solid nutrition.
- Take one last look at the cycling position.
- Put on your wetsuit. Now you're getting down to business.
- Short swim warm-up.
- Starting signal! Don't get lost and stay calm despite the thick crowd. Nothing is decided in the first 500 yards.
- First transition, don't waste time, things are going great, hurry up!
- Cycling, solid ground at last; drink every 10 minutes, eat and drink every 15 minutes. 2 ounces of carbohydrates per hour is a lot but it has to be done.

- Now there's only the running to go! Find your running rhythm, stay relaxed, drink and enjoy yourself. Compensate for moments of weakness by slowing the pace. Short walking breaks at the refreshment stations allow you to get your strength back. Another 10, 9, 8, 7, 6, 5, 4, now only 3 miles.

- What a blast. The finishing line has come too soon, what a shame.

- The finish, the cheers and excitement are unforgettable.

- I am an Ironman 70.3, and now belong to the illustrious circle of Ironmen and -women.

- I am proud of myself: My long awaited dream has come true.

www.chris-herzog.ch

What next?

You can and should make this IRONMAN 70.3 or medium distance dream come true more than once. As for whether or not this challenge can still be interesting the nth time around, here is a short story from Henry.

After my Ironman Austria in 11:19 h at the beginning of July, the best season of all starts for me: A vacation and recovery from triathlon challenges at the same time. For years, I have sworn by doing endurance fitness training after an Ironman, but only relaxed and enjoyable endurance training with several fellow vacation guests from the Anderwald Camp site at the wonderful, warm Faaker Lake in Carinthia, Austria.

As a display case was dedicated to me on June 20, 2007, in the German Sports and Olympia Museum in Cologne, Germany, and the finish of the Cologne Triathlon is situated directly in front of the museum, I planned to contest my 250th triathlon there. After competing over two medium or Ironman 70.3 distance triathlons at the end of May and beginning of June, both in 5:16h, it made complete sense for me to complete my third medium distance of the year there.

S. Aschwer

The organizers planned a special tribute for me: 100 yards before the finish line, I was to change my running shoes for the ones that were in the museum. They were the original running shoes from my first Hawaii Ironman in 1985. I was to cross the finish line in front of the museum with these running shoes from 1985, and then take them straight back to the museum.

After competing in nine triathlons in the 2007 season, and a few running races, I was a little stale mentally, but looking forward to Cologne, back in 1984, I had contested a distance that was somewhat longer than the modern medium distance in a water temperature of 57° F and without a Neoprene wetsuit. My great idea of wearing one of our daughter's bathing suits to protect against the cold water was always laughed at. Perhaps I was the pioneer for the modern triathlon outfit, I always say with a smile.

I started in Cologne at 7:25am. 5:35 hrs was my target race time, and I arrived at the museum at exactly 1pm. A delayed course inspection by the city of Cologne led to a 50-minute delay to the start, which was to take place with 600 participants in the 66° F Fuehlinger Lake. This delay got on quite a few triathletes' nerves. I was not so bothered because my Neoprene suit was warm.

With my teammate Peter, who was contesting his first medium distance, we joked a little: "Boys and girls, please! This isn't surgery, it's only a triathlon."

At last, the starting signal sounded. I have tried to have as little physical contact as possible in the water since I broke my toe in Almere, Netherlands, in 1985. Now it's every man for himself, even my teammate Peter. I wouldn't have minded running a few miles with this thoroughly fun-loving triathlete, who was exclusively a strength athlete until three years ago and therefore has a few problems with the running. A nice swimming course here on the regatta course, 0.77 miles there and back. At 1.5 miles, it was a little longer than in the Ironman 70.3, but it didn't matter.

It was not the green water that suddenly bothered me but water in my goggles. I had definitely replaced my swimming goggles on my swim cap, I thought to myself anxiously. I immediately tried to get rid of this small problem and pushed the edge of my swim cap. I kept on swimming, feeling like a water polo player. Keep on going, Cologne is calling. I was already imagining the beautiful running course around the lake and then along the Rhine into the city of Cologne. But first Henry you still have to cycle for 56 miles. Somehow I would do it, although after the Ironman I had badly neglected my cycling.

Again, I think back to 1984. That was my test for Hawaii, I remembered it vividly. If I survive Cologne, then I will tackle Hawaii, I said at the time.

Now I was able to enjoy it to the fullest and appreciate getting out of the water and moving on to the cycling. 56 miles, a long training ride on flat terrain, which was not my favorite.

So what? I am a triathlete and can go with the flow. I get out of the water after 48:30 minutes, but it's ok. I can still use my energy in the cycling and running. I am brimming with anticipation. I change my clothes completely in the transition zone. This procedure takes me six minutes, as in this cold weather I don't want to go without drying myself off or my compression socks that I have been wearing for several months now. At my age, these support socks are necessary. They give me a positive, powerful sensation, both on the bike and on foot.

On the bike, out through the spectator cordon, against the wind and the 56 miles. Annoyingly for me on the cycling course there were many groups. I got into an argument twice because I noticed that 5-6 triathletes were cycling in my slipstream. "Boys, at the finish there are lollipops for you, a gobstopper and no finisher t-shirt, you should enter the Cologne Guilt Cycling Race or do you already need the slipstream of a 60 year-old man," I shouted a few times.

People should not be that lazy. There is enough room for everyone. Peter seems to be getting on well. I can always recognize him at the turning points by his white knee socks. A lot of jovial banter when overtaking, or even when being overtaken, makes the time fly. Only using high gears, I am back again after 2:40 hrs. Everything is going according to plan A.

The second transition is a bit quicker, although I again take the time to change completely. Wearing relaxed running clothing, I am finally on the move again. Today, running is my favorite discipline, in the Ironman it is cycling, in Linz, Austria, in the medium distance it was swimming in the 75° F Pleschinger Lake. Never mind, a glance at my watch tells me that there is still 1:55 h to go until the little performance at the museum. I can't feel any trace of the supposed race fatigue of the last 10 days. I am completely in my element, in my race comfort zone, at a heart rate of 132-133 in the medium distance. In the Ironman it was only 129. Today I'm sure must give hope to countless youngsters. I run the first 4.4 miles around Fühlinger Lake in the overtaking lane. With every ray of sunshine, I feel better and better. We runners were cheered by a group of seniors who were walking around the lake with walking sticks. Thank you, thank you, I reply. To a young athlete, whom I quickly overtook, I encouraged him: "Come on, we can do it, that is my age group that is cheering us on," I said. Not arrogantly, just because I was so happy to still be able to run so relaxed. After running through the forest for a while, we enter the Rheinaue wetlands.

It is simply awesome to have come this far and to have avoided the massive hoopla of Hamburg in the World Championships. In triathlon I prefer natural surroundings, not so much the noisy cities. Even after the fast lane, the miles continue to fly by. I can maintain my tempo of almost exactly 8 min/mile without any problem. "Isn't that crazy?" I ask myself. Today is my tenth triathlon in the season that is now ending, and I have had no problems of any kind in any competition.

It is unbelievable! Perhaps it is because it is my 25th triathlon season, that I enjoy it so much. There is definitely also the added excitement of measuring myself against others in competition. I say competition deliberately and not battle, because for me, a triathlon is not the place for a fight. The only fight is against the course or the outside conditions, not other fellow athletes.

Here my job is to swim, cycle and run, and I am grateful that I can do it. Countless unforgettable events associated with the triathlon run through my head and through my whole body, and I am humbled by them. In 25 years I have had so many lovely experiences, positive craziness, and met so many nice, fantastic athletes. I am also thankful that I am able to pass on many tips, advice and suggestions from these times in my books, and be a mentor, advisor and motivator. Despite all of this, I would never have dreamt how things would work out 25 years later. The great flood of personal mail encourages me to continue.

At the same time, I enjoy watching old father Rhine flowing along and run quickly towards the Cologne cathedral. There, at km 19, I am way ahead of schedule. The barriers are placed closer and closer, and it is more and more difficult to overtake. Maybe the organizers did not expect people to still be overtaking at this stage of the race. However, I still feel as strong as before, strong and fast enough to overtake a few more participants. The fact that they are all youngsters encourages me even more. I take my earplugs out of a small pocket and push them into my ears, against the expected noise of the finish. Then the last sections: Two runners just in front of me. You can get both of them, I am sure. With long strides I cover the last few hundred yards to the finish. I hear the loudspeakers and the crowd. Where are my Hawaii shoes? Nowhere to be seen. I am apparently

10 minutes too early, but I continue striding on and suddenly find myself at the finish line and run through it, where my friend Georg Kröger and my family take me in their arms.

I am moved, just grateful. I can't speak. My moist eyes say it all.
    Now for the interview.
    "Thank you, thank you. The running course was just too short for me," are my first words!

Only 5:24 hrs have passed and I have already finished. What a shame that everything is over so quickly.

My personal summary:
What fascinates me in the triathlon is measuring myself against other people and the conscious enjoyment of the swimming, cycling and running courses!

10.3 Regeneration

Post-race nutrition

The finish line at the end of the race is also the starting line for the next one and where regeneration begins. This consists of replacing water, minerals, trace elements and vitamins as quickly as possible. You should also make sure you rebuild depleted protein reserves. The same naturally also applies for nutrition after a hard workout.

After an intensive endurance performance, the muscles' receptivity to carbohydrates is increased. The recovery process is accelerated by refilling the glycogen reserves. Our metabolism is still heightened for days after the performance (afterburn effect), and even if we are not very active, we will need to eat more than normal.

Athletes who have little appetite after a race will find high-carb drinks or soups useful. They allow the athlete to both quench their thirst and consume electrolytes and carbohydrates. The normalization of electrolyte and protein balances can take a few days depending on the amount of effort expended. During this time, you should try to consume potassium – and magnesium – rich food, i.e., plenty of vegetables, fruit, cereals, pulses and dried fruit, eggs, milk, meat and fish.

Don't forget trace elements either, like iron and copper. Unfortunately, these days, natural mineral water alone is not sufficient to compensate for the losses, as iron has been removed for reasons of taste and appearance. Also choose drinks that contain trace elements like low-fat milk drinks or pure buttermilk. It is advisable to supplement with a low-dose a mineral and trace element mixture. After a post-race meal, that puts little stress on your digestive tract, high-fiber food is recommended for the next few days.

Quite a few triathletes long for a nice cold beer after the race. Alcohol is absorbed very quickly by the body, but also quickly excreted, so alcohol cannot be used to replace lost fluids. This means that before the beer (if possible, alcohol-free) you should drink something else first. Alcohol also prolongs the regeneration process.

10.4 The return to training

After the successful finish, you should plan the rest of the season with pride. You will have had many personal experiences upon which you can draw in future races. It is definitely true that we must experience certain things ourselves in order to be able to internalize and use them on a lasting basis. We can read about something 10 times and not really pay attention to it. A triathlete must have first-hand personal experiences – both positive and negative – in order for memories to "stick." We authors cannot protect some readers from making mistakes; we just hope that our book helps reduce these problems.

H. Ash

Triathletes who have only been practicing endurance sports for one, two or three years, or athletes in their 40s or 50s should enjoy a phase of active rest during the two weeks after the race. Especially in the first regeneration week, try to avoid running and just do a little cycling and/or swimming, or even some other light exercises.

In the second week, you should return to gentle training in each discipline. From the third week onward, start the rebuilding process with a normal training week.

Experienced triathletes can return to normal training after only one week following a 70.3 race. In the 2007 season, Henry only needed one week for an almost complete regeneration, in order to complete an Ironman 70.3 in exactly the same time as the previous week. This was probably due to his 30-years'-plus endurance training background and the fact that he never goes flat out in races.

During the rebuilding phase, it is important to analyze previous training and the results achieved. The athlete's whole environment should also be reviewed. Where are the strengths, where are the weaknesses, what can be improved?

New goals after an Ironman 70.3

- Improve your time in future races.

- Master an Ironman 70.3 with a particularly difficult cycling or running course.

- Tackle a full Ironman.

- Experience other Ironman 70.3 events worldwide.

- Qualify for the World Championships in Clearwater Beach, Florida.

- Win your age group in an Ironman 70.3 or medium distance.

- Simply enjoy competing over new triathlon courses in different countries.

- Prepare for a new Ironman 70.3 with a family member, a training group or a club.

- The fact that there are outstanding triathlons all over the world should inspire your imagination and longing for new athletic goals. All these suggestions apply to both young and old triathletes.

H. Ash

11 The Experience of "Flow"

Have you ever had the feeling that everything went smoothly, that time flowed like a river, that you just felt good and wanted to "hug the world" out of happiness?

If you can answer "yes" to these questions, you were in the flow. This is an indescribable high, as though you are floating on clouds and at one with yourself and with the world.

11.1 What is "flow"?

Flow describes the process of flowing from one moment to the next. Mihály Csíkszentmihályi created the notion of flow. He observed the phenomenon of flow in completely different areas of human activity, such as chess, rock climbing and rock'n'roll dancing.

11.2 Recreational activities

If you tried to earn your living by playing chess, rock climbing or rock'n'roll dancing, you would unfortunately realize that this is an unlikely career move. Our society could not survive for long either if all its members were devoted themselves to only such "recreational" activities. The activities researched by Csíkszentmihályi are characterized by a very strong internal (intrinsic) motivation.

11.3 Triathlon and flow experiences

In triathlon, there are frequently moments that give us joy and trigger feelings of euphoria, too. You may know the high after working when, despite a hard day at work, you pull on your cycling or running shoes in order to get a few miles in. Or you drive to the swimming pool just to swim a few lengths or to refine your swimming technique. A wave of euphoria spreads throughout your body, and you just feel absolutely great.

You can find yourself in "flow" during training and competition. During a race you go through different phases, and sometimes you may not feel so good. Your arms and legs feel heavy and your body aches with every movement. Then, from one moment to the next, everything suddenly runs relaxed and smoothly, and you master the course with unaccustomed ease. One thing is certain: it doesn't matter whether you have participated in a short triathlon or an Ironman 70.3, you will experience highs at some point. Most people find that the euphoria appears immediately, others find it only sets in a few days later when you fully realize what you have accomplished. In any case, you know that by finishing successfully you have achieved something special.

11.4 The nine elements of flow

According to Csíkszentmihályi – the founder of flow research – there are nine main elements, which are examined below with examples from the world of triathlon. Flow experiences occur in training and competition, which is why both areas are considered for each point. You may read something you recognize here and identify with one or more elements. Or you may experience similar moments in the coming weeks and months that will remind you of these nine flow points:

1. **In every phase of the process, there is a clear goal:** In flow, the person concerned knows exactly what his goal is. A musician knows which notes he must play next, a surgeon knows how he must make the next cut, and a farmer has a set plan for growing his crop.

   Flow in training
   As a triathlete, you can give a lot of variety to your training with swimming, cycling and running. For running, be careful with the surface; you know where you have to put your feet so that you don't trip. If you plan to run a 5-mile circuit as a training run, you also know where and how you will run this distance. If you have a training plan, your goal may not only be set in terms of mileage but also by accurate mileage splits (e.g., 9 minutes/mile).

   Flow in competition
   In a competition, as a triathlete you also know exactly which discipline follows the other. You have a goal before you and know how to approach it step-by-step in order to be a successful Ironman 70.3 finisher.

2. **There is direct and immediate feedback to your actions:** When expriencing flow, a person knows they're doing well. The musician hears immediately whether he is playing the right notes, the surgeon notices straight away that no blood is flowing into the abdominal cavity and the farmer sees the straight furrows in his field.

   Flow in training
   You will immediately feel whether your arms and legs are fresh and whether you can perform your workout relaxed and lightly. These

are usually the days when things are going well. When everything is good in your private and professional life, it will be reflected in your training.

Flow in competition

In triathlon, you also get immediate feedback if things are going well. When swimming, in the middle of the jostling crowd, you can hold your ground so that you don't go under. When cycling, you soon notice whether the tempo is right or whether you must get off your bike prematurely. The same applies during running: If the tempo is right, then you can manage to run the 13.1 miles. But if you start too fast, then you can still try to walk to the finish, to reach the goal, otherwise you may have to give up.

3. **There is a balance between challenge and ability:** In flow, there is a balanced relationship between one's abilities and the task at hand. In a game of tennis, a player may become frustrated because his opponent is too strong and powerful; the other player may be bored because he cannot fulfill his potential. The ideal scenario is a tennis match where both players walk a fine line between challenge and boredom.

Flow in training

In a training group, you should make sure that you know your fellow athletes' ability level. If the group is too strong, you will be out of your league and get frustrated because the tempo is too fast. You even run the risk of getting injured or not enjoying the triathlon. The reverse is the case if the tempo of the group is too slow. You will eventually get bored because you are not really challenged. You should therefore look for a training group whose performance level is similar to yours. Even if you train alone, you may struggle with a hilly course or a tempo that is too fast. If you always cover the same course at the same speed, you will get bored. You should therefore make sure you change your training routes and speed from time to time.

Flow in competition

During a competition, you may become frustrated if you realize that for whatever reason (lack of training, overly fast race tempo) you have to drop out. You will rarely get bored in a triathlon race if you are able to set your own pace and become an Ironman 70.3 finisher.

4. **Action and awareness merge:** In flow, everything is focused on the activity itself. A nurse who is measuring blood pressure concentrates on the job at hand and temporarily forgets about the other problems.

Flow in training
When you pull on your running shoes, focus only on tying them up. Breathe deeply and shake off any negative thoughts. Now try to concentrate on running and pay attention to your breathing.

Flow in competition
In a competition, you have to concentrate on different movement sequences. For swimming, this means that you must be aware of how you catch the water with your hands and then pull through with a powerful arm action. In running, this means that you concentrate on placing your feet correctly and letting your hands swing relaxed. You are mentally absorbed in the action of running and don't worry about your rivals or think about family or professional problems.

Pepe Kuess

5. **Concentration blocks out distractions:** It is important to concentrate on the task at hand. If a musician worries about his tax problems while performing a piece of music, he will probably play a wrong note. The surgeon who is distracted during an operation may place the patient's life at risk.

Flow in training

While you are running, you must always be aware of the surface underfoot, especially if you like to run on dirt roads or in the forest. If you start thinking about your family problems while you are running up a mountain, you could fall and seriously injure yourself. Avoid distracting thoughts and concentrate on the present moment! That is not quite as easy as it sounds.

Flow in competition

In a race, you should not worry about your problems either, but instead concentrate on the competition. There will always be time to address these problems later.

6. **Do not fear failing:** During the flow experience, you will be too preoccupied to contemplate failure. You feel that you have everything under control.

Flow in training

You should not be afraid of failing in training. If you train alone, it is up to you to decide how far and how fast you run. There is no need to pressure yourself to succeed. If you follow a training schedule, it doesn't mean that you have "failed" if you don't manage to complete the planned workout.

Flow in competition

During a Competition, you would not contemplate giving up. You would concentrate completely on each movement. Your ability corresponds to the challenge; you are at one with yourself and sure you can accomplish your goal.

7. **A loss of self-consciousness:** In flow, you are not worried about making a positive impression on others. In a flow state, you have the feeling that you can transcend your own limits and temporarily be part of a greater whole.

Flow in training

If you manage to forget yourself as you cycle or run through the countryside and not to think about other people, then you are in flow. Perhaps you have already had this experience during a run and everything just felt right.

Flow in competition

In an Ironman 70.3, once you have crossed the finish line after 70.3 miles, you will feel that you have accomplished something special and, that you have discovered your own limits of suffering and performance.

8. **Loss of a sense of time:** Time is irrelevant in flow, and hours can pass as fast as minutes. The opposite can also occur. For instance, figure skaters have reported that a fast spin seemed to last 10 times longer than it did in reality. The sense of time is distorted, and the subjective experience of time does not correspond to the actual time.

Flow in training

You may be familiar with the following situation: After a long workout you just jump into the water. What seems like minutes later, you get out again. What has happened? You were in a state of flow. Your training time flew by and you lost sense of time and it seemed to you that you were only swimming for a few minutes instead of an hour.

Flow in competition

In an ideal competition, it happens that time runs away with itself and you seem to reach the finish faster. If you have problems running, the closing half marathon run can become a half marathon walk in which time seems to stand still and you never seem to get any closer to the finish.

9. **Autotelic activity:** Activities are autotelic if there is no reason to practice them other than that they improve one's quality of life. In everyday life, most activities are exotelic, as they simply have to be done to achieve a mundane aim, such as earning money. A musician who is paid to play and still loves his work lives a fulfilled life.

Flow in training

Most of your activities are exotelic, because you must work to earn money so that you and your family can survive. The percentage of people who are lucky enough to make a living off of triathlons is very small. You don't have to do triathlons; this sport is classified as a recreational activity. However, the combination of the three sports helps you to improve your life. You are sick less often, can eat what you like, maintain your weight and just feel absolutely great.

Flow in competition

Completing an Ironman 70.3 is an autotelic activity. There is no particular reason to do it, apart from the above-mentioned improved quality of life. Nevertheless, thousands of people every year choose to experience the very intense suffering and indescribable joy that is the triathlon.

W. Freidl

11.5 The danger of flow

There is the danger of becoming addicted to the flow experience. The simple beauty of the deep flow world is so seductive that many triathletes withdraw from everyday life in order to pursue their sport in this private, self-contained world. To do this is to lose the constructive potential of flow. Tension between the flow experience and personal experience is absolutely essential if the former is to enrich the latter.

So, don't neglect your family and friends, stay in touch with your environment, for there is more to life than triathlon training and competition!

Finally, here are a few practical tips for your flow experience:

- Enjoy every step in training; try to be at one with yourself and your surroundings.

- Once you have tied your laces, leave your problems (as much as you can) behind you and concentrate only on running.

- If you are training in a group, make sure that your colleagues have a similar ability level to you otherwise you will be out of your league or unchallenged.

- Block out distractions when training and competing, and don't think about professional or personal problems.

- When you are swimming, concentrate only on swimming, or when running think only about running, let your arms swing relaxed and place your feet one in front of the other.

- Don't even think about failing: you are already under pressure to succeed in both your professional and private life.

- Don't let others talk you out of doing triathlons. It is true that you won't earn a living doing it but it will clearly improve your quality of life.

- Don't just give up after the first few miles if you still have not experienced flow yet. It will come and you may even run a personal record time!

K. Reitenbach

12 On Your Mark, Get Set, Go! Motivation Tips

The mental starting signal has been given: On your mark, get set, go! The following motivation tips will help you on your way to becoming an Ironman 70.3 finisher. Let us first just repeat a few comments on how it should not be done. Examples of triathletes' inappropriate behavior can often be seen after a competition.

Triathletes who are unhappy with their performance have an excuse for everything during the race: the weather was too bad, the wind too strong, the mountain too long or too high, the water too cold, the weather too hot, the swimming too crowded, the water too rough, the swimming time too slow, the transition went wrong, too many cyclists on the course, the food was no good, there was no cola, the usual food was not available, their legs were too heavy, the cycling split was just too long, the running course was too difficult, the road surface was not fast, the form wasn't good, the just-healed injury, the missing running cap, the course was too long, the lost age group victory, the just-missed qualifying time, etc.

Athletes can come up with a thousand excuses. We often have the impression that some athletes are talking about a different race. If we think that every triathlete has put in plenty of time for his or her training and paid a lot of money for the equipment and traveling expenses, and despite finishing, can find the craziest reasons for his or her supposed failure, then something is wrong with their mental attitude.

In a triathlon that extends over 70.3 miles, sometimes the stupidest problems can occur. It is this struggle against these uncertainties and difficulties that helps to make us into "Iron" men and women. Henry can tell you a thing or two about this with his 250 triathlon starts.

As Mark Allen once said:
"Triathlon is not just a sport, it's a way of life!"

Although during the 2007 season I completed two Ironman 70.3 races within eight days, another half distance at the end of the season, an awesome Ironman in Klagenfurt, Austria (with an average heart rate of 129) and a series of other Olympic distance races, I really experienced no problems at all. Expect worrying! This may have been because I always really looked forward to the races and always stayed within my "race comfort zone" during them. Or it is simply that after 25 years I have become so laid back that nothing can disturb me now? Henry has already been through enough problems, particularly in 36 Ironman races. There is not enough space to list them all here.

This very complex area, in which a healthy tension and a positive attitude are very helpful, is described very well with a statement from triathlete Detlef Graewe. His attitude is clear in his relaxed comment one hour before an Ironman:

> "I have no idea why triathletes are all so nervous; this is not surgery, but the most beautiful day of the year that we have all been looking forward to for so long!"

Often, we have no control over unexpected difficulties and problems and just have to deal with them. Remember: "For every problem, there is a solution," and we can always control our attitude.

12.1 Mental motivation tips

You have now been training for a while and may have taken part in the occasional small competition. Now you wonder whether you could manage an Ironman 70.3. You will definitely do it, and a few motivation tips will help you on your way.

First, it is important that you set a goal, such as successfully finishing an Ironman 70.3.

Imagine the following: You are a sailboat. A sailboat needs wind (motivation). The direction this boat sails in depends on whether the sail is set correctly and the rudder is in the right position. If sail and rudder are set correctly, the boat will sail with the force of the wind. You may have a lot of energy, but if your activity is not optimally directed, you will sail in the wrong direction or move around aimlessly.

You should initially set only one goal, for if you have too many balls in the air, you will lose them all. In practical terms, this means that you sign up for an Ironman 70.3 that takes place in one year's time. You then have 12 months to prepare for this race. The "wind," or the motivation, is reaching the finish line, and you will train for this moment for a whole year (hopefully with enjoyment).

The three different disciplines bring variety to your everyday training, thus giving your boat momentum. Also set a realistic timeframe in which your goal can be accomplished (e.g., the above-mentioned 12 months for a successful Ironman 70.3 finish).

During your trip with the sailboat, you will go through phases with more or less wind (motivation). If your motivation is flagging, imagine how happy you will be when you have accomplished your goal. It can be an image of you crossing the finish line, in which you are cheered on by your friends and family pleased that you have managed to combine your training with your family, and professional life. You may have an image all by yourself running your favorite course in a personal record time and how happy you would be. Always keep this image in your mind's eye if your sailboat comes to a standstill.

On your journey, you will also experience storms that threaten to capsize your sailboat. Don't let your boat tip over: there is always a way out of the crisis. One of these crises could be that you have gotten injured in training and worry that you can no longer follow your journey to being a successful Ironman 70.3 finisher. Give yourself time for the injury to heal, for if you force things, you will surely fail and your boat will capsize. You lose nothing if you postpone your goal. Simply accept this setback. While you are off training due to injury, remember that many athletes come back stronger after a forced break. Be patient, even if it is hard for you, and keep your sailboat in a safe harbor for a while. When you are fit again, you can take your boat out, set sail and go out to sea with renewed strength. You will see how quickly you regain your old form after a few weeks and are still able to take part in the race as planned.

Just one more tip: During your voyage with the boat don't forget your crew and include them in your plans. If your crew includes your family and friends, then talk to them about how they can support you on your journey. Some days you may not feel like training, and then it can definitely help if your crew reminds you of your goal so that your boat can get back on course.

A few more practical tips for a successful Ironman 70.3 finish:

- Set one goal; if you have too many balls in the air at the same time, you will drop them all.

- Goals give purpose and meaning to your activities, as well as motivation.

- Set a realistic timeframe for the goal you want to accomplish.

- When you are not feeling motivated, imagine your goals.

- If you are injured, take time to heal properly as this will make you stronger and quicker.

- Don't forget your family and friends on your quest to success.

With this, we wish you enough wind on your sailing journey: Set your sail and rudder correctly so that you always keep going and you will soon be part of the "great family" of Ironman 70.3 finishers.

12.2 A short motivational story

Never give up!

A short motivational story to finish with, not from us but from a blind man's audiotape.

Marlies is a semi-professional triathlete. She also works half-days for a blind man. He went blind at the age of eight, like his brothers. There are many causes for the blindness. The fact is that all three guys must live with their blindness and accept their limitations. Marlies' boss is a masseur by profession, and in his free time often goes for bike rides with partners on a tandem. He also has a running partner who picks him up, takes him by the hand or elbow and takes him running. As a blind man, he listens to a lot of audiotapes in order to find out what is going on around him.

He gave one of these tapes to Marlies to listen to, and she heard a wonderful inspirational story, which motivated her to become an Ironman 70.3 finisher:

Three frogs came across a jug of cream. Without further ado, they jumped into the jar as it looked like heaven to them. They swam enthusiastically in the jug and drank until their little stomachs were full. When they were satisfied, they wanted to get out of the jug. Only then did they realize with horror that the walls of the jug were too high and too slippery to get out. When they realized that they were in a hopeless situation, two of the frogs gave up, sank to the bottom and drowned. However, the third frog had learned never to give up. He struggled and flailed about with all his might, but the apparent hopelessness made his strength slowly disappear. He then kicked one more time with all his might and redoubled his efforts. He struggled even harder and suddenly the cream turned into butter, the frog had found something to stand on and was able to jump out of the jug.

What an inspiring message for a future Ironman 70.3 finisher! Never give up, no matter how hopeless the situation may seem, for there is a solution to every problem.

We wish you health and success on your journey, and may your cream turn into butter!

M. Nüsken

Appendix

The eight levels of training intensity:

The following descriptions and abbreviations are used for the different training intensities:

Percentage of HRmax	General description of training levels	Abbreviations of training levels
100	Race pace 3 miles running, 13 miles cycling and 550 yards swimming	T8
95	Very hard training	T7
90	Hard training	T6
85	Very quick, fast training	T5
80	Quick training	T4
75	Relaxed training	T3
70	Gentle training	T2
65	Very gentle training Regeneration training	T1

Low intensity endurance	65-75% HRmax
Medium intensity endurance	75-85% HRmax
High Intensity endurance	85-95% HRmax
Maximal	› 95% HRmax

The distribution of training intensities in the competition period

Training level	Ironman 70.3 Beginner (B)	Ironman 70.3 Ambitious (A)	Ironman 70.3 Performance oriented (P)
T1 Reg.	15%	10%	5%
T2			
T3	80%	70%	70%
T4			
T5			
T6	5%	20%	20%
T7			
T8			5%

The distribution of training volume

For our training plans, we use the following approximate distribution of training volume in four weekly training cycles:

Week 1	Week 2	Week 3	Week 4
Normal week	Normal+ week	Hard week	Regeneration week

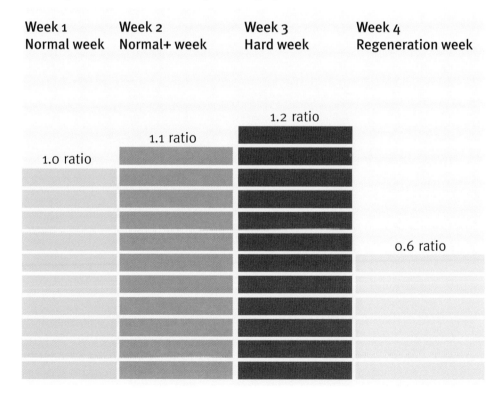

1.0 ratio   1.1 ratio   1.2 ratio   0.6 ratio

Further Reading

Aschwer, H. (2000): *The Complete Guide to Triathlon Training*. Meyer & Meyer, Oxford.

Ash, H. & Warren, B. (2003): *Lifelong Success. Training for Masters*. Meyer & Meyer, Oxford.

Aschwer, H. (2001): *Tips for Success – Triathlon*. Meyer & Meyer, Oxford.

Aschwer, H. (2002): *El Entrenamiento Del Triathlon*. Paidotribo, Barcelona.

Ash, H. & Warren, B. (2004): *Lifelong Training. Advanced Training for Masters*. Meyer & Meyer, Oxford.

Ash, H. & Warren, B. (2005): *Triathlon Exito de por vida*. Tutor, Madrid.

Himmerich, C. (2005): *Keep Fit Exercises for Kids*. Meyer & Meyer, Oxford.

Internet Addresses:

www.HermannAschwer.de
www.Marlies-Penker.at

www.Ironmanlive.com
www.Ironman.com

Photo Credits:

Cover design: Sabine Groten
Cover photo: Imago Sportfotodienst
Jacket photos: Bakke-Svensson
Other photos: see captions

IRONMAN®
The Triathlon Edition

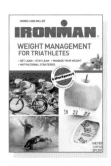